Eat! Eat!

Eat! Eat!

*Wonderful Recipes from the Old Country
Like My Mother Used to Make*

Ruth Kanin

DONALD I. FINE, INC.

New York

Library of Congress Catalogue Card Number: 94-68102

ISBN: 1-55611-433-8

Manufactured in the United States of America

10   9   8   7   6   5   4   3   2   1

Designed by Irving Perkins Associates

Dedicated to—who else?
Sadie Kanin: 1890–1979

Acknowledgements

With gratitude and appreciation to the following:

Donald I. Fine, my publisher, for his understanding and support of my book.

Bob Gales, associate publisher and marketing director, for being so warm and friendly in helping to guide me through this project.

Larry Bernstein, production director, whose expertise is the tops and cooperative manner so enjoyable.

Jason Poston, associate editor, so efficient and such a good person.

Karen Berman, cookbook editor, for her conscientious and expert suggestions in tune with me and my book.

Bernard Shir-Cliff, literary agent extraordinaire, for his patience, encouragement, practical help and ideas—a joy to work with.

Natalie Silverman, P.Dt., of Montreal, professional dietitian, for being so generous with her time and savvy in the diet section.

Susan Asanovic, M.S., R.D. of Connecticut, registered dietitian, for her valued contribution to diet information.

My favorite tasters and testers, my friends Mary Hoffman, Pauline Shapiro and Charlotte Sonshine, and for the good times we had feasting.

Robert Duplessis and his many relatives who appreciated my recipes, proving that even Québécois can like Jewish food (even at Christmas dinners), especially my rice pudding.

Janine Déschênes, another French friend introduced to the mysteries of Jewish cuisine and learning to like it.

My brother Garson and sister-in-law Marian, who were so helpful in many wonderful ways from cheerleading to professional advice and exceptional efforts. My thanks and love.

My daughters Cass and Dena, who have happily scarfed down their grandmother's and mother's food, including the vegetables, for over four decades.

Contents

Fish   39

Poultry   51

Meats   63

Vegetables 79

Potatoes, Noodles, Rice, and More 89

Salads 103

Noshes or Snacks 113

Breads 125

Desserts 135

Menus   155

Information   163

A Note to Canadian Readers

Please be aware that Canadian all-purpose flour is different from American all-purpose flour and will not work the same way in many recipes, especially when baking. The biggest difference occurs with active dry yeast. Canadian flour is made from hard wheat (about 95 to 100%) and American flour contains about 75% hard and 25% soft wheat. Hard wheat has more gluten (a protein).

What this means in cooking is that you will use *about* 2 tablespoons *less* per cup of Canadian flour, but this is not a foolproof formula. (Adapting recipes depends on the other ingredients used as well.) For example, for a yeast bread recipe that calls for 5 to 6 cups of all-purpose flour, you may need only 4 to 4 1/4 cups flour to get the same result. *But you will need to experiment with each recipe.* Start with a smaller amount of flour and add more gradually until your dough or batter is the right consistency. Dough should be soft and pliable, until it just stops sticking to your fingers. Also, Canadian flour absorbs more liquid, so you may need to increase the amount of liquid.

Introduction:
My Mother, the Chef

My mother was 81 when she came to stay with me one summer. I am disciplined, organized and a schedule-person. She was the opposite. The odds were against my completing a summer course toward a master's degree, so I had to think quickly. Mom was famous for her food, and I had wanted to collect all of her recipes for some time. Many were from her Lithuanian background, a few from friends, and most were her own inventions and adaptations. My father was Russian, so many of his favorites were in her repertoire.

So I planned a project—on a schedule. We would write a recipe book. We would cook every afternoon from two to five o'clock.

It worked, except for one thing: Mom couldn't deal with measurements. She didn't even own measuring equipment. But she agreed to cope with this for the sake of our book. Her culinary training took place in an era when recipes called for a "wine-glass" of milk or "for three cents challah" from the *Jewish Daily Forward,* her favorite newspaper. Like most traditional cooks, she clung to her *sheet arein* method (throw it in—or cooking-by-ear). In that, she was sister to home cooks in other times and places who were unhampered by home economists and cooking by rules (e.g., the 18th century New England housewife who wrote in her leather-bound family book in a florid hand, "Specific instructions for Indian Pudding: Take the morning's milking and throw into it as much corn meal as you can hold in your hand. Let the molasses drip in as you sing one verse of 'Nearer My God To Thee,' but sing two verses in cold weather." A hundred years later a southern black woman improved and simplified this method of pouring molasses from a jug: "Put in three glunks . . .").

In dispensing with the skills of ad-lib cookery, we have also dispensed with much charm, individuality, flair and abandon. But it's also true that to cook by ear, one must have apprenticed hundreds of hours to know when a batter feels right, or to intuitively judge time and temperature.

So how come I didn't already have Mom's recipes? A good question. My own early lack of free-style skill was not altogether my fault. She didn't like me fooling around in the kitchen when I was little, fearful that I would chop off a finger or two. The 'cooking' I was usually allowed to do was to set the table and stir the soup, provided I didn't get too close to the flame, and even then she would hover over me to make sure my dress didn't catch fire. This attitude never changed, even after I had two kids of my own, but as I grew older I managed to cook with her from time to time, getting a few recipes, and tolerating her warnings about death traps that lurked in an ordinary kitchen.

That summer, when I began to tackle the project of getting the recipes down in modern measures, and as I stood with pencil poised, the instructions ran something like this:

MATZO BALLS

"Put the matzo mell in a bowl. Make a hole and break in the eggs."

"Wait a minute, Mom, how much mell?"

"Oh, maybe half a box."

"Which size box?"

"I forgot. I think the big one." (I go get the box and check the amount.)

"Okay, and how many eggs?"

"Two is good, or even four is better if you got."

"How many did you put in now?"

"Three."

"Okay, Mom, go ahead."

"Put in a little from the chicken fetz . . ."

"How much, exactly?"

"Exactly? . . . Oh (figuring carefully and weighing an imaginary amount in her hand)—enough."

I soon realized the only way was to follow her through the making of each dish, to grab her arm as she was about to put whatever-it-was in a bowl and to measure it before she could get it in. But often we would have to go through the whole process again because she would sneak in a pinch or a spoonful more of something as she went along, automatically tasting and feeling, usually when my back was turned. If I would object, she would counter-accuse: "Mrs. Measurement!"

But I finally got her:

We had arrived at a blintz batter that she declared perfect by the feel of it as it dripped from a ladle. It was an even measure, fit for any modern cookbook. We made over a hundred blintzes with a variety of fillings. They were marvelous. After all, she had been making them for over 65 years. But just before she left to go and lie down, she turned to me and said, "Listen, Rutele, you'll write me down the recipe." We shared this joke for years.

To see that other people enjoyed these recipes as much as we did, we had tasting parties and until everyone said that the borscht or rice pudding, etc., was the best they tasted, it didn't go into the book.

So here, already, is our recipe book. Along with the countless friends and relatives who shared her food, come and join us.

Jewish Type Food

Ours was not a kosher kitchen since my parents were not particularly religious. But having been raised in an orthodox home, my mother was imprinted with certain rules. Like most of her *landsleit* she would not touch anything from a pig, or any shellfish, and would not combine meat with milk products, claiming it unhealthy.

Kosher cooking is ritually clean by dietary laws with details so intricate that over 400 orthodox points must be carried out with two sets of dishes, for *milkhech* or *fleisheig*.

But it's traditional for non-ritualistic Jews to respect the orthodox. When my super-*froom*, (super-religious) Bubbeh Dena came to live with us, Mom kept strict kosher for her and never cheated even a little. When kosher or even semi-kosher friends ate with us, there was never anything *treif*, or not kosher, on the table, such as butter with meat.

If you are a stranger to Jewish food, you may be inclined to think of it as heavy, greasy and indigestible. Wrong. Only heavy-handed cooks, Jewish or otherwise, cook like that. But you will get heartburn if you pig-out—excuse the expression—whenever delicious Jewish food is around. It is as superb a cuisine as any.

The varieties are infinite, depending on ethnic origin whether Hungarian, Russian, German, Lithuanian, etc. We are noted for our ability to adapt to the country of our choice. It also narrows down to which block your mother lived on in the old *shtetl*. I once witnessed a ferocious argument between Mom and her best friend over which way to fold *kreplach:* oblong or triangular.

Ingredients are often exotic and recall Biblical text: ginger, cinnamon, honey, pomegranates and persimmons. Other typicals are chicken fat, kasha, hard-boiled eggs, matzo meal, poppy seeds, sour cream, fresh noodles, prunes, cream cheese, lox, herring, borscht, pot roast and great breads: sour rye, corn rye, egg twist, onion, pumpernickel and luscious cakes, cookies and pastries.

But don't try to find a Jewish steak. There is no such animal. Dietary laws prevent the use of the hindquarters (unless purified by near-impossible ritual), also the aging of meats, so unless meat is ready to fall apart, as my mother warned me, it is not sanitary or edible. Many old-time recipes, in fact, read, "cook until meat falls from bones."

If you are like me, you will find tradition fun and maybe nostalgic. Whether these recipes stir old memories or create new ones, good food and feelings go together—like bagels with cream cheese and lox.

A Few Notes
About This Book

All recipes are designed to serve six people with generous portions unless it says otherwise.

People like things more or less salty. I notice that in some books the amount of salt called for would be too much for me. The recipes here are less salty than most, but it was the way we liked them, and today's nutritionists and doctors advise cutting down. Most recipes will therefore say "salt and pepper to taste" but some recipes will specify an amount. So use your own judgement, but if you want to add more, start with a little and work up.

About Lithuanians. An origin-unknown friendly feud exists between the Litvaks—Jews who lived in Lithuania—and Galitzianers—Jews who lived in the region known as Galicia (now Poland). Litvaks are ridiculed mainly for their accent. For example, we reverse the *sh* and *s* sounds, so some of the dishes will appear in phonetic spelling different from yours, but don't give me a hard time about which is correct. Any way you learned it is right.

About Lithuanian food, in addition to classic Jewish food, we adopted and adapted some Russian, Polish and Scandinavian dishes, such as herrings. We share the Baltic, after all.

Important

All regular flour in this book refers to the pre-sifted, all-purpose flour. If other flours are used, it will be indicated whether it is to be sifted.

We used extra-large eggs. (See the "Hints" section, p. 166, on how to adjust egg sizes.)

We used unsalted butter—if you use salted, use a little less salt in the recipes.

My mother didn't mind using my measuring equipment—that was the point—but she was used to her old meat grinder and little shallow wooden chopping bowl and little curved chopping knife. But when I made some of the dishes on my own, I used my food processor, electric rice cooker and blender. If the recipe says to grind, either way will work.

Please don't forget to check the "Cooking Methods" section (p. 163) if you're not sure about how to do something.

Advice to Dieters
of All Types

There are all kinds of diet books: low fat, low sugar, low salt, low cholesterol, high fiber, allergy control, low-cal for weight loss, anti-aging, a dizzying variety of diet plans, etc., etc. It's enough to make you crazy. My mother didn't know from such things. For instance, she had a no-frills attitude toward fat people: "They eat too much."

She herself was a little *zaftig*, a complimentary term meaning attractively full-figured. Men of her generation would say that they liked a woman with a little meat on her bones (some still do). But Mom was not fat and rarely sick. One reason is that she was physically active and this is in tune with today's fitness advice. Instead of saying, "I'll go down to the store," or "I'm going to Becky's" (her sister), she would say "I'll run down to the store" or "I'll run over to Becky's." She did everything fast.

In her day fitness was not the giant industry it is today, and certainly scientific experiments have made tremendous strides. Millions of lives are saved by new knowledge and advice that keeps emerging. The print and electronic media concern with fitness and health keep us up to date with torrents of information about the good news and the bad news about our health. I just hope we will not go overboard and lose the simple pleasures of cooking and eating by focusing on fears and guilts and complexities connected with food.

Since this is a personal book and not diet-focused, I will offer you advice I have gleaned from today's health and diet *mavens* that could help you adapt the recipes in this book to approved nutritional standards. So don't turn me in for practicing medicine without a license.

The only problem is that these *mavens* don't agree all the time, and new studies are constantly being made that shift or replace these standards. So I'll offer you a range of options in some cases, and for fun, I sneaked in some tricks I have learned or developed through the years that work for me.

Fats: Some people want to cut down on fat to lose weight, now that stout is out and thin is in, and some are told by their doctors to cut *out* fat completely for medical reasons. If you've got a high cholesterol count, it's saturated (hardened) fat that is bad for you, mostly found in animal fats, but also in coconut and palm oils. You would need a Ph.D. in biochemistry to understand the details—so if you just remember that monounsaturated and polyunsaturated vegetable oils are okay, and even help reduce cholesterol level, that's enough. A few of these are safflower, sunflower, olive, canola, and corn oils. BUT they should be used in moderation, and be aware that there is the same number of calories in any form of fat. Another point to remember is that fat calories are denser than others. One gram of fat equals nine calories, while one gram of protein or carbohydrate equals four calories.

So how can we watch our fats and *still* cook traditional Jewish dishes? There are some ways.

Jewish cooking isn't Jewish without *shmaltz* (chicken fat). Nothing tastes quite like it in cooking with one exception: a product called Nyafat, only you may have to search for it in Jewish markets. It's not healthier than chicken fat because it's saturated. The only advantages are the taste, and because it's a vegetable fat, it's *pareve*, which means it can be used for both milk and meat dishes, a boon to kosher cooks. Another way to use *shmaltz* with a surprisingly good result is to use only a touch of it with a healthful oil. Even a teaspoon or two will give you a little of the flavor.

The use of margarine as a substitute for butter is one subject where lots of *mavens* disagree. So you will have to choose sides. Anti-margarine people say that in the process of hardening oil (hydrogenating) to make it spreadable, a saturated trans-fatty acid is formed which is a factor in heart disease. But producers of margarine began to experiment and developed a process that doesn't have that result. And here is a big BUT again: use only the soft kind that comes in little tubs; look for the good oils in it, and avoid any with coconut or palm oil. It should have 50% or more of the polyunsaturated and monounsaturated oil than the saturated. So become a careful label-reader if you decide to use this product.

If you want to cut down on butter and use more oil, you can make what I call Butter Plus: put a pound of butter in a big bowl with 2/3 to one cup of safflower oil. Wait until the butter is soft, then whip it until smooth. If you add one or two tablespoons of powdered skim milk it will be more spreadable. Put it into containers and, if you wish, keep one out and freeze the rest. You will still have a nice butter taste and it will be easier to spread. This way you have the benefit of safflower oil which has the highest percentage of linoleic acid, and essential fatty acid which is necessary in the metabolic process. Sunflower or other oils that you like will work too.

To eliminate butter entirely, there are butter substitutes that you sprinkle on foods.

Many recipes will work with less fat, and it's been found that traditional recipes have used more fat than is necessary to get a good result, so you can cut the fat by a third. Oil can substitute for butter in many recipes, but use about a quarter less oil. A new idea is to use applesauce for half the fat. A nice plus in this trick is that the applesauce is sweeter and thinner than oil, so you can reduce the sugar and add more flour. But experiment to get the taste you like.

To cut fat in frying, the non-stick pans are excellent. Vegetable-oil sprays work nicely, too. But if you use fat, use a good oil and brush it on the pan with a pastry brush. Sometimes baking can substitute for frying.

As for milk products, there is always skim milk instead of whole milk. Buttermilk and low-fat yogurt can be used in some types of recipes. Again, it pays to experiment.

Cream is marketed now in a range of milk fat content: 10%, 12%, 15%, and 35%. The 12% to 15% is what some recipes call half and half (half milk and half cream). There is good news about substitutes for the beloved whipped cream: a hand blender with a special whipping attachment will make a reasonable facsimile of whipped cream from skim milk—and it will taste good if you add a little powdered sugar or sweetener. It can also be flavored with vanilla or other extracts or fruit juice.

I have seen 1% MF (milk fat) sour cream in most markets now. In many recipes low fat yogurt, sweetened a bit, will substitute for sour cream.

Cream cheese is available with reduced fat content as is cottage cheese. I have seen versions of cottage cheese as low as 1% MF, even 1/4 of 1% and a surprisingly tasty one with no fat at all.

Eggs: Even on low-cholesterol diets, a couple of eggs a week are usually allowed. (The whites are not restricted—it's the yolks that have a very high cholesterol content.) Egg substitutes can be found in most markets in the freezer section. Better yet is to use two real egg whites in place of one egg in recipes. You can make a good omelet with only whites if you perk it up with other things like onions, chopped bell peppers, tomatoes, or whatever strikes your fancy.

NOTE: I have a secret that I use when I find myself with too many leftover yolks. I beat them up with a little olive oil and lemon juice to a paste and guess what? Work it into my hair and leave it in for about an hour before a shower. It's a good protein treatment and gives my hair a nice shine.

Sugar, etc: If you need to use less or no sugar, this can be tricky because there is hidden sugar in most prepared products, so you will have to become a label-reader.

But in home cooking, many recipes will work with less sugar. Some experts say that sugar is sugar no matter what form, even honey. And this is another area where the *mavens* clash. Health food people usually defend honey, even claim it has healing effects, provided it's pure. What can I tell you? We're talking Jewish cooking here, and so many Jewish cooks would get mad at me if I advised them to stop using honey, a favorite ingredient in lots of recipes and a welcome guest at holiday meals and rituals. But again, realize it is a form of sugar, and use it sparingly to be on the safe side.

Another trick for using less refined sugar is to substitute concentrated frozen *sugarless* fruit juices, and I have found a number of delicious sugarless jams and jellies. But remember, these are highly concentrated, so go easy.

Imitation sweeteners are forbidden by many *mavens*. They think they are dangerous. Some people are allergic to them. So here we go again, bogged down by controversy—because other *mavens* recommend them, particularly in medical cases like diabetes and hypoglycemia.

Some of the sweetener manufacturers offer their product in a bulk format which has the same sweetness as sugar, so it can be substituted in equal amounts. But it's not the same sweetness as in the little packets you put in your beverages, so watch out.

With sugar and its substitutes, to use or not to use is up to you and your doctor. But everyone agrees that you should try to use less and to control that sweet tooth.

Salt: If you have high blood pressure, you have probably been advised to cut down on salt. It's also a factor in weight gain. There are salt substitutes and some nice tasting seasoning salts, but the flavors may take getting used to. Begin by using less salt and wean yourself off much or all of it—a little at a time. Substitute herbs and spices, lemon juice and vinegar. Any dish with lots of onions doesn't need salt. Most recipes in this book will work with less or no salt.

Meat, Poultry and Fish: I would be insulting you if I advised you to buy extra-lean ground beef. But it's good to know that it cuts the fat dramatically. The best choice, though, is to do what my mother did: buy lean cuts, and have your butcher trim all the fat off the meat before grinding it for you, or do this yourself at home. It's a snap if you have a processor. Veal and chicken and turkey breasts are good low-fat choices. Removing the skins cuts fat about in half. You can go even further if you put your *cooked* meats or poultry in the refrigerator until the fat solidifies, then just pick it off.

The choices of fish are vast and most are low in fat. A few of the lowest are sole, cod, flounder, pike, halibut, and haddock. Salmon and trout are among the fattest, but they contain valuable fatty acids called Omega-3 which reduce cholesterol and inhibit blood clots. They have more calories, though, if you are watching these carefully. And if you buy canned fish, check labels carefully for oil and salt content.

One of the best ways to cut down on animal fat is to use more legumes (beans, peas, lentils) which have the double advantage of being high in protein and fiber.

Fiber (in Mom's day it was called roughage) has become famous in the last two decades as an important element in good health, particularly digestion. The best known sources are fruits, vegetables and whole grains. How much to eat and what kind depends on the individual, so figure it out with literature on the subject or with an advisor. If you need to add more fiber, you can adapt the recipes by using whole grain flours, and sneak more fruits and vegetables into dishes. For example, add whole grains and/or vegetables to a portion of ground beef dishes, soups, salads, and stuffings.

We should, of course, watch what we eat, but I hope you will not become obsessed with dieting or fearful of every bite. If you want to change your eating habits, do it gradually, so you will not feel deprived. After a while, you won't miss your old eating habits. Finally, watch your weight and don't neglect to move your tush—exercise is essential to good health.

Appetizers

Cooks are usually opinionated on the subject of
appetizers—what kind to serve, whether to serve
them hot or cold, or whether to serve them at all.
Mom couldn't understand little pieces of food.
Famous for quantity as well as quality, even when
she lived alone she cooked enough for at least ten
people. Appetizers to her were part of the meal, and
a mountain of chopped liver was the norm for
guests. Itsy-bitsy things on crackers were usually
done by me or guests-helpers. But now and then her
artistic urge would inspire her to stuff celery or
arrange crackers with spreads on a tray and con one
of us into going around and making sure that
guests were properly stuffing themselves.

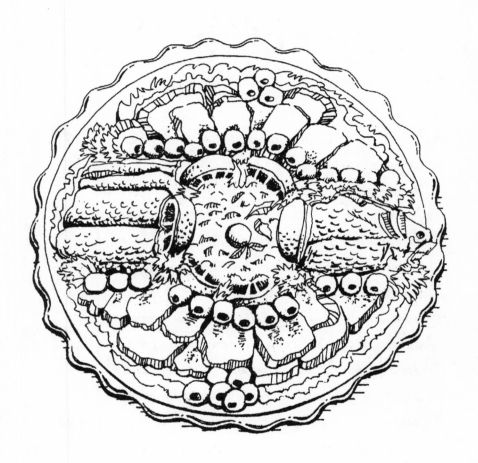

Chopped Liver

Serves about 12 people unless you are inviting some big fressers

Chopped liver is a real drag to make, but worth it since it's always a favorite at company dinners or even family meals. Among our relatives and friends there was an ongoing competition for best recipe. I've tried them all and kept going back to Mom's.

The secret is plenty of onions and chicken fat, but you can use less of either of those if you prefer and adjust the seasonings—more or less salt or garlic. You can also soften the texture to your taste by adding more broth.

Jewish cooks are usually rigid in their preference for one kind or combination of liver: all chicken liver, all calf's, or our favorite, half and half. But I've found that it's all good, even if—God forbid—you should mix in some pork liver. But please, don't blame me if my chopped liver isn't your chopped liver.

Which reminds me. Through the years, chopped liver has gotten a bad rap from the so-called joke: "What am I—chopped liver?" I don't know who started it. Probably somebody whose mother was a lousy cook. But it's a major treat, worthy of the pride French gourmet chefs have in their pâtés.

Note: *The secret of tender texture is to broil the liver until the rawness is just cooked out and it's still pink and soft. The actual chopping of the liver can be done by hand or with a meat grinder or food processor.*

1 pound liver (get a little more, like 1/4 pound, if it has a lot of membranes, as you will cut these out)	1/4 cup chicken fat
	2 hard boiled extra-large eggs
	1/2 to 1 teaspoon salt
	Pinch of pepper or paprika
3 medium onions, peeled and sliced	Pinch of garlic powder

Preheat the broiler. Broil liver until it is pink and soft. (Chicken liver takes about 5 minutes; beef or calf liver takes a few minutes more, depending on thickness.) Remove liver from the broiler and set aside.

In a large frying pan, heat fat over low heat. Add onions and sauté until golden brown and tender. Stir often—this may take 30 minutes or longer, depending on the onions.

If you are using a grinder, grind the liver, onions and egg together.

If you are using a food processor, first remove the membranes from the liver and then process it alone, until it is coarsely ground; it should *not* be pureed to a paste. Remove the liver from the processor and transfer it to a large mixing bowl. Next, process the egg whites, and add them to the liver. Finally, process the onions and add them to the liver mixture. In a separate bowl, mash the egg yolks and add them to the liver mixture.

Once the liver, eggs and onions have been coarsely ground, add the salt, pepper or paprika and garlic powder. Mix until well combined. Taste and adjust the seasonings if necessary.

The traditional way to serve chopped liver is in a nice bowl on a platter, surrounded with crackers and a variety of Jewish breads. Try thin-sliced pumpernickel or rye cut into little fingers and toasted lightly for easier spreading. To make it pretty, add extra hard-boiled eggs, yolks and whites mashed separately, and make a design on top.

Chopped Herring

Makes about 1 cup

Now and then I get a yen for a salty taste, and nothing else will do but some chopped herring on melba toast or plain crackers, or even as a sandwich with a tomato and cucumber slice.

In the old days, chopped herring was hard to make. We had to go to a special store where herring was kept in big barrels; you took it home wrapped in newspaper. We used *matjes* or *schmaltz* herring (very, very salty), filleted it, then soaked it to get some of the heavy saltiness out. If you can't find whole herring any place, the prepared products in glass jars are a good close-runner. Try the different brands until you hit the flavor you like. It should be salty, though. That's the idea. If you don't get a three-hour heartburn at least, you're not making it right.

1 slice white bread
2 tablespoons wine vinegar
1 hard-boiled egg
1 large sour apple, peeled and
  cored
1 stalk celery, finely minced,
  optional
1 (8-ounce) jar herring fillets
  or 1/2 pound filleted salty
  herring

1/2 small onion, or use the
  onions from herring jar
1/2 teaspoon sugar, or more as
  needed
Sliced tomato, optional, for
  garnish
Sliced cucumber, optional, for
  garnish

Soak bread in wine vinegar and mash in egg yolk. Grind or coarsely chop apple and onion and, if you wish, celery. Add herring and continue to chop, then add egg white and chop again. Add to bread and egg yolk mixture, add sugar and mix well. It should have the texture of coarse cornmeal, not a paste. Serve on crackers or in sandwiches.

Garnish with tomato and cucumber slices if you wish.

Little Herring Kneidlach— Litvish Style

Makes about 3 dozen

I remembered these herring dumplings from my childhood, along with delicacies such as *eiter* (cubed and baked cow's udder, alas, no longer available). But Mom hadn't bothered with herring kneidlach for years, so for our cooking project, we experimented with the recipe; it took four tries to recapture the taste I recalled. The tastes and smells of childhood are powerful. Marcel Proust's *Remembrance of Things Past* was triggered by the aroma of a *madeleine*. Herring kneidlach did the same for me, bringing an entire joyful period of my early life into sharper focus.

1 cup (about 8 ounces)
  prepared herring fillets
1/2 medium onion
1 extra-large egg
1/2 cup matzo meal

2 teaspoons white vinegar
1 teaspoon sugar
Pinch of pepper
Sliced cucumber, optional, for
  garnish

Using a hand chopper or grinder, coarsely chop the herring and onion. Transfer to a large mixing bowl. Beat the egg with a fork and add it to the herring mixture. Add rest of matzo meal, vinegar, sugar and pepper and mix until well combined. Refrigerate for 30 minutes.

To cook the kneidlach, bring a big pot of water to a simmer. Then, rolling the batter in the palms of your hands, make little balls the size of large Concord grapes. Drop each dumpling gently into the simmering water and cook for about 15 minutes. Cool and serve with toothpicks.

Note: *The flavor of these kneidlach will vary with the saltiness of the fish. Herring in a jar is usually not overly salted, but if you buy herring in a fish store, you may have to soak it in water before cooking unless you like it that way. So taste the batter and adjust as you go. A touch more sugar if you wish.*

You can also make larger balls, cut them in half and serve over a thin slice of cucumber.

Easy Blini, Plain or Fancy Shmancy

Makes 24 blini

I came across a cookbook by a descendent of the hateful Czar. She referred to sour cream as crude food favored only by peasants. I told Mom about that and it made her mad. I suggested that we show *her* (she had been long dead) and we threw a fancy Russian dinner party using sour cream in every dish, from blini to cheesecake. It was a memorable party, famous for years.

These blini take a while and require lots of watching, but you can make stacks and stacks, freezing an extra supply. They warm up beautifully, right from the freezer in a 350° oven.

We served them cold, with bowls of sour cream, chopped hard-boiled eggs—yolks and whites served separately—minced onions, scallions or chives and red and black caviar. Little wedges of lemons and limes look gorgeous. If you have room on the table, you can add herring pieces (in wine sauce) or eggplant caviar. Arranged artistically on a silver platter, it's the imperial traditional way. Mom called it *pish-pish* (double pish means very, very ritzy).

At our famous party, one sour note came when a guest saun-tered into the kitchen, his plate piled high with blini, and asked, "Y'got any maple syrup?" Needless to say, he was never again invited to a blini party. Maple syrup is great in its place, but not on traditional Russian blini.

1 tablespoon unsalted butter
1 1/2 cups milk, or more as needed, scalded and cooled to lukewarm temperature

1 cup prepared buckwheat pancake mix
1 extra-large egg, well beaten
1/4 cup sour cream
Enough vegetable oil for frying

In a large mixing bowl, melt butter in warm milk. Add pancake mix, egg and sour cream and mix until all ingredients are well combined.

In a large frying pan or griddle, heat oil over medium heat. Ladle out enough batter so that blini are about 3 inches in diame-ter and about 3/l6 inch thick. If batter seems too thick, add a little more milk. If it seems too thin, add a bit more pancake mix.

When blini bubble and undersides are golden brown, turn over and gently press down with a pancake turner. When they are light golden brown on the other side, remove from the heat at once—otherwise they get too tough. Mind you, these are not plump pancakes—they are more like pliable crackers.

Old-fashioned Blini, a Harder Way

Makes about 50 blini

If you are a purist and willing to bother, here's a recipe for tradi-tional blini. They are thinner, more tart—a slightly different product.

1 ounce yeast
1/2 cup unsalted butter
1/2 cup plus 3 1/2 cups milk, or more as needed, scalded and cooled to lukewarm temperature
4 extra-large eggs

2 cups buckwheat flour, sifted
2 cups all-purpose flour
3 to 4 tablespoons sugar
2 teaspoons salt
1/2 cup sour cream
Enough vegetable oil for frying

Dissolve yeast in 1/2 cup of warm milk. In a separate bowl, melt butter in 3 1/2 cups milk. Separate eggs, and beat yolks and whites.

In a large mixing bowl, combine flours, sugar and salt. Add milk, butter and yeast mixture. Mix well. Let stand for 1 to 2 hours. Add sour cream and egg yolks and mix. Finally, fold in egg whites. Let batter stand for another 15 minutes. The batter should be on the thin side, so if it seems too thick, add 2 to 4 tablespoons more milk. Taste and adjust the flavorings.

In a large frying pan or griddle, heat oil over medium heat. Ladle out enough batter so that blini are about 3 inches in diameter and about 3/16 inch thick. Reduce the heat to low and cook for 2 to 3 minutes, until blini begin to bubble. Turn and continue cooking for about 2 more minutes, until undersides are light golden brown; watch carefully, adjusting flame to keep them from getting too brown, but making sure they are well cooked.

Note: *Buckwheat flour will vary in taste, so try one blini as a sample and adjust the flavorings as desired.*

Chopped Eggs and Olives

Makes 2 1/2 to 3 cups

These next two mixtures are very versatile and can even be meals in themselves for a light luncheon salad. I often serve a generous scoop of one or the other on a bed of lettuce with rings of pineapple, quartered and scalloped around it, each scallop topped by a strawberry.

If you read ahead, you have probably figured out that the onions and olives can be mixed together for a third mixture.

These are ideal for stuffing celery, cherry tomatoes, or spread on crackers.

6 extra-large eggs, hard-boiled and mashed

2 cups (16 ounces) canned black olives, pitted and minced

4 to 6 tablespoons mayonnaise

Salt and pepper—easy does it

Pinch of grated nutmeg, optional

Pinch of mace, optional

Mix together. It's best to mix in the eggs while they are still warm.
Serve in a bowl by itself, or on a platter surrounded by slices of tomato, cucumber or whatever your heart desires.

Chopped Eggs and Onions

Makes about 2 1/2 cups

6 extra-large eggs, hard-boiled
and mashed
1 medium onion, minced fine

1/4 cup mayonnaise, or 2
tablespoons mayonnaise and
2 tablespoons sour cream

Mix together while eggs are still warm. Serve on a platter surrounded by potato chips or crackers and topped with strips of anchovy fillets, or in celery stalks.

Eggs Stuffed with Lox

Makes 24 stuffed eggs

Lox was always expensive, but even when it became exorbitant in price, my mother didn't believe in economizing on food. But once when she was helping me with a brunch party, she insisted that Sunday brunch must have lox and cream cheese with bagels. I would only go for a ridiculous amount such as 1/8 pound. She rose to the occasion and together we made these toothsome nibbles. Everyone loved them, but she still thought I was cheap.

12 extra-large eggs, hard-boiled
3 ounces cream cheese
2 to 3 tablespoons milk
2 to 4 ounces (1/4 to 1/2 cup)
lox

3 tablespoons finely minced
scallions
1 scallion, cut into 1-inch
strips, for garnish

Cut eggs in half. Arrange whites on a platter. Mash yolks. Soften cheese with milk. Mince lox and mix it with scallions and cheese. Combine mashed yolks with cream cheese and carefully stuff whites with the mixture. Trim with remaining strips of scallion.

Baked Matzo Cheese Fingers

Makes 12

We liked these tasty "fingers" plain, but you can play around with different flavorings, for example, cinnamon, nuts, jelly. Be creative.

Note: *If matzo is pre-salted or flavored, you might not want to add salt, so serve it on the side.*

3 ounces cream cheese
2 tablespoons minced or grated onion, or more if desired
2 to 3 tablespoons milk, if needed

2 matzos
Salt, optional
2 tablespoons melted unsalted butter, or more if desired

Preheat the broiler.

Combine cheese and onion, softening the mixture with milk if needed to make it soft and spreadable.

Spread each matzo with cheese mixture, covering the entire top, including the corners so they won't burn. Matzo breaks easily, so be careful.

Brush with melted butter and sprinkle with more onion if desired. Place matzos on a broiler rack.

Broil for about 3 minutes, until they are lightly browned on top. Watch them carefully to keep the matzos from burning.

Remove matzos from the broiler and gently slide them onto a platter. Cut into 2-by-3 inch "fingers" while they're still warm. They will get stiff when cool. Serve hot or cold.

Cream Cheese Creations

I hope you will agree that cream cheese is an endless source of inspiration and taste. I like to make trays of nibbles and pass them around, because some guests don't like to get up and down for appetizers. Mom thought they should serve themselves, but quite often I would see her going around and stuffing her creations right into people's mouths.

Here are a few variations. Try them; then create your own.

Spreads:

3 ounces cream cheese
2 to 3 tablespoons milk
Soften cream cheese with milk and mix with any of the following:
—6 black olives and 1 table-spoon onion, all minced

—1/4 cup chopped lox
—3 or more tablespoons chopped walnuts and 2 tablespoons raspberry jam

Serving Suggestions:

—Spread plain cream cheese on thin-sliced pumpernickel (the kind that comes in squares). Cut into "fingers" or little squares. Make a pretty design on top with anchovy fillets and slices of pimento-stuffed green olives.
—Quarter cherry tomatoes halfway down but do not cut them through. Put a dab of olive-onion spread on top.
—Spread round crackers with cream cheese, cover with thin slices of cucumber and garnish with olive slices or bits of anchovy.
—Stuff celery with any spread.
—Buy or bake mini bagels (half the size of regular ones) and spread with lox and cream cheese mix. Or spread cream cheese thick and fashion a lox design on top.

Raisins and Almonds

This fruit and nut mixture has a special place in the hearts of Eastern European Jews and their descendants the world over. Once you have heard it, you'll never forget the haunting Yiddish folk lullaby with the refrain, *"Rozhinkes mit Mandlen,"* or "Raisins and Almonds." Even without this song, however, the combination makes a tasty treat.

Mix raisins and almonds together in a pretty dish. If you like, you can steam the raisins a few minutes to soften them. The almonds are usually peeled. To peel them yourself, boil them in water until you can slip off the skins easily.

Soups

Soup is a funny thing. It's an emotional food. For instance, in cold weather, there is nothing like a bowl of hearty, hot soup with bread and butter to warm you in body and spirit. And we all know the nurturing reputation of chicken soup.

But back in Sha'at, the shtetl my mother came from, it was a matter of economics. Soup was eaten every day because it used up every scrap of food and was cheap and filling.

When I was growing up, it was taken for granted as a part of every meal. Jewish meals have lots of courses. But an added feature for Mom was that it was a great way to sneak in extra things to fatten us up, like cream and eggs.

We'll begin, of course, with the soup that is synonymous with Jewish Motherhood.

Chicken Soup with Matzo Balls

Serves 6

You can make a decent facsimile of chicken soup with a good canned stock or powdered broth, but no Jewish cook worth her salt (or his) would stoop so low. Make it from scratch with a nice fat chicken.

Chicken Soup:

1 (5 to 6 pound) roaster, cut up
1/2 medium onion, peeled and left whole
1 large carrot, peeled and left whole

1 large stalk celery
1 1/2 teaspoons salt
2 quarts water, or more if needed
6 large or 12 small matzo balls

Place chicken, onion, carrot and celery into a large big pot and cover with 2 quarts of water. Add salt, cover and bring to a simmer. Cook for 1 hour, uncover and continue cooking for another hour; add more water if needed. Cook until chicken is tender, but not falling off the bones.

Let stand until cool. Remove chicken and vegetables from soup. Mash onion and return it to the pot. Strain the soup into a large bowl.

The fat can be fully removed by leaving the soup in the refrigerator until the fat solidifies on the top. It can then be skimmed off—but do save it to use in other recipes.

Cut up vegetables into bite-sized pieces to serve, or leave the soup clear. Serve hot with matzo balls.

Matzo Balls:

Makes 6 large or 12 small matzo balls

3 extra-large eggs
1/4 cup chicken fat
1 teaspoon salt
1/2 teaspoon sugar
1/2 cup chicken soup

1/2 teaspoon dried parsley
Pinch of grated nutmeg, optional
1 cup matzo meal

Beat eggs well. Melt fat in a small saucepan and transfer it to a large mixing bowl. Add salt, sugar, eggs, broth, parsley and, if you wish, nutmeg. Add matzo meal, mix well and let stand for at least 30 minutes. The batter will absorb the liquid, expand and thicken.

In a large saucepan, bring about 2 quarts water to a simmer. Then, keeping your hands wet, shape batter into 6 dumplings the size and shape of small baked potatoes. Or make 12 small, round ones. Drop dumplings into simmering liquid and simmer uncovered for about 20 or 30 minutes, depending on size.

Sickbed Soup

Serves an invalid 2 to 3 times, depending on hunger

We all know chicken soup is famous as the "Jewish penicillin"— science has recently declared that there is a healing agent in it. But how many people know about milk soup? It is what I was always given when I was sick in bed. Don't ask me why. It was one of my mother's remedies for invalids, which is what you were considered after one sneeze. Come to think of it, milk and honey acts as a tranquilizer, and rest and sleep do heal.

2 cups milk	Salt
1/4 cup cooked rice	Honey

In a medium saucepan, heat milk and rice over low heat. Add salt and honey to taste.

Variation: *If you like your soup a little thick, make a thin white sauce first: in a medium saucepan, heat 1 teaspoon unsalted butter and stir in 1 teaspoon of flour. Cook over low heat until the mixture bubbles. Then slowly add milk. The more flour and butter, the thicker the soup.*

Lentil Soup with Kosher Frankfurters

Serves 6

Everybody's collection should have a good lentil soup. This is one of the best I ever tasted. It's one of those comforting soups for a cold winter day.

1 tablespoon vegetable oil
1/2 onion, chopped
6 cups chicken broth
2 cups dried lentils, soaked in
   water overnight or for at
   least 4 hours
2 stalks celery, with tops, cut
   in small pieces

1 carrot, diced
1/2 teaspoon thyme
1/2 teaspoon rosemary
1 teaspoon salt
3 kosher frankfurters, cut in
   1-inch cubes

In a big pot, heat oil over medium heat. Add onion and saute for about 5 minutes, until it is translucent but not brown.

Add 6 cups broth. Add lentils, celery, carrot, thyme, rosemary and salt and bring to a simmer. Cover and cook for 1 hour. Add franks and simmer for another hour or so, until lentils are soft enough to mash with a fork.

Remove franks from the soup. Cool the soup and transfer it, in batches if necessary, to a food processor. Process until the soup is thick and smooth or put through strainer. Return soup to the pot, add franks, heat and serve.

Variation: Instead of chunks, use only 1 frank, slice it thinly and fry slices in a little vegetable oil until they are brown and crisp. Float slices in each bowl as decoration. Add croutons if desired.

Cold Lithuanian
Beet Borscht

Serves 6

For years, I wasn't sure whether this particular borscht recipe is distinctive of Lithuanian soups or not. I heard so many arguments pro and con. But all the Litvaks I've known use the following ingredients, especially the hot potato touch.

The flavor is tricky to achieve and there is no way to describe the special sweet and sour taste required for a true cold borscht. If you have never tasted it, you are better off starting with canned pickled beets, and if you want a sharper taste, add more sugar, lemon juice, vinegar and salt. Another option is to buy a bottle of ready-made borscht where Jewish products are sold and sample it—memorize the taste. Long ago, we used *sour salt* as flavoring, a special product not readily available today, but recently I saw it among the spices in a gourmet delicatessen. But the following is a good start with ingredients probably on your shelf now.

Note: *I cut fresh beets on a platter to avoid staining my board.*

2 to 3 cups (1 to 1 1/2 pounds) fresh cooked or canned beets, julienne or grated

1 to 1 1/2 quarts water (including liquid from canned or boiled beets)

1 to 2 tablespoons white vinegar, or more as needed

1 to 2 tablespoons lemon juice, or more as needed

1/2 to 1 teaspoon salt, or more as needed

1/2 to 1 teaspoon sugar, or more as needed

3 medium potatoes, peeled and cut in half

1/2 cucumber, peeled and cut into bite-sized pieces

3 extra-large eggs, hard-boiled and coarsely chopped or cut in half lengthwise

1 cup sour cream

If you are using fresh beets, peel, cover with water and cook over medium heat until soft. Reserve cooking liquid. Cut beets up, put them into a big pot, cover with water and cooking liquid, and add vinegar, lemon juice, salt and sugar.

Simmer for 5 minutes. Taste and add more of any of the flavorings, if needed. Cool and chill.

Bring another saucepan of water to a boil, add potatoes and cook until very soft.

To serve, ladle out 6 portions, evenly distributing beets. Divide cucumber and eggs between the bowls and top each with a dollop of sour cream. Just before you are ready to eat, place a piece of hot potato into each bowl.

Fresh Tomato and Rice Soup

Serves 6

My kids and I loved the taste of stewed canned tomatoes and sometimes we made them into a soup by just adding water. Mom thought canned foods would kill you slowly, so she developed this recipe to save our lives.

2 tablespoons unsalted butter
2 tablespoons minced onion
2 tablespoons minced celery
1 small clove garlic, mashed
2 tablespoons minced green
   bell pepper
2 tablespoons flour
6 tomatoes, peeled and cut up

6 cups water, or more if
   needed
1/2 teaspoon salt
1 teaspoon sugar
2 teaspoons lemon juice
1 cup cooked rice
Sweet cream for serving

In a big pot, heat butter over medium-low heat, being careful not to burn it. Add onion, celery, garlic and green pepper and cook for 5 minutes, stirring often. Add flour and saute for about 3 minutes or so.

Add tomatoes and water and simmer, covered, for 1 hour, or until all vegetables are very soft. Strain vegetables and soup into a large bowl, mashing vegetables through the strainer with the back of a ladle or wooden spoon. If you have a food processor, of course, it's easier. Add salt, sugar and lemon juice and adjust the taste if necessary. Add more water if needed.

Return soup to the pot, add the rice and heat. Serve with a swirl of sweet cream in each bowl.

Split Pea Soup,
Fussy and Easy Methods

Serves 6

Personally, I find the making of split pea soup from scratch a pain in the neck. (You have to soak the split peas for at least 4 hours, drain and discard the soaking liquid.) The canned variety suits me fine, but if someone makes me a pot the harder way, I'll admit it does taste deliciously better.

Split Pea Soup, the Fussy Method:

1 cup green split peas, soaked
   in water at least 4 hours
1/2 onion, sliced
2 quarts plus 1 1/2 cups water,
   divided
1 teaspoon salt, or more as
   needed

Black pepper
3 tablespoons unsalted
   butter
3 tablespoons flour
6 matzo balls, page 27
Sweet cream for serving

Pour soaked split peas into a big pot. Add the onion and cover with 2 quarts water. Season with salt and pepper, and simmer until the split peas and onion are very soft. This might take as long as 2 hours. Taste and adjust the seasonings.

Transfer the soup and vegetables to a food processor and process until thick and smooth. Or strain the soup and vegetables into a large bowl, mashing the vegetables through a strainer with the back of a ladle or wooden spoon.

Rinse the pot, add the butter and heat over medium heat, being careful not to burn it. Stir in the flour and saute until it bubbles, then add 1 1/2 cups water slowly, stirring constantly to avoid lumps. (If you miss any, lumps can be removed with a wire whisk if necessary.)

To serve, divide the soup evenly between 6 bowls and place a large matzo ball in each. Swirl a tablespoon of cream around the matzo balls.

Split Pea Soup, the Easy Method:

2 (16- or 17-ounce) cans pea
soup (2 cups), diluted with 2
cups water
1 (16- or 17-ounce) can

chicken consomme (2 cups),
diluted with 1 cup water
2 tablespoons chicken fat or
unsalted butter

In a big pot, heat the diluted pea soup, consomme and fat or butter over medium heat. Proceed as above. Don't use cream with this one if you keep kosher, because it contains chicken consomme.

Potato-Oatmeal Soup

Serves 6

Speaking of emotional, this is a soup I remember eating all my life. It's a classic peasant soup, and when I get too snooty, it reminds me of my humble beginnings. It also happens to be delicious, filling, very nutritious, and costs less than peanuts.

2 cups steel-cut oats (not
rolled oats)
8 cups water
3 medium potatoes, peeled
and cut into 1-inch cubes

Salt
Cream for serving
Sunflower seeds, optional, for
garnish

Boil the water, add oats, reduce heat and simmer for 15 minutes. Add the potatoes and simmer about 30 minutes longer, or until the oats and potatoes are soft, but not too soft. The oats should be slightly crunchy, and the potatoes tender when pierced with the tip of a sharp knife.

To serve, swirl some cream on top. Sprinkle with sunflower seeds if you like.

Barley and Mushroom Soup

Serves 6

Here is another comforting soup. Invite a troubled friend over for a bowl and see how it picks up her spirits.

Actually, it's got everything: protein, carbohydrate and vegetables. With some toasted challah and pure sweet butter (the only kind ever allowed in our house) it's a satisfying meal and then some.

1 cup pearl barley	2 carrots, sliced
1 cup dehydrated mushrooms	1 stalk celery, thinly sliced
12 cups chicken broth	Sweet cream or milk for
1 teaspoon salt	serving

Soak barley overnight. Pour boiling water over mushrooms and soak them overnight, too. When you are ready to cook the soup, drain both and discard the soaking water. (You might have to change the water several times.) Cut mushrooms into small pieces and transfer them and the barley to a big pot.

Add broth and the salt and bring to a simmer. Cook for 1/2 to 1 1/2 hours, until soft.

Meanwhile, in a separate saucepan over medium heat, cook carrots and celery in enough water to cover until they are almost soft. Drain and add to soup and continue to cook for another 20 to 30 minutes, until all ingredients are very soft.

If the soup is too thick, add more broth if needed to make it thinner. Swirl a little milk or cream on top before serving.

Note: The taste of this soup will depend on the flavor of the broth. You can use homemade chicken broth or the powdered store-bought kind. There are many variations of this soup. Some add lima beans, onions or even chunks of meat. But we like it the simple way, as above. With a hearty bread and a salad it makes a gorgeous meal.

Capoosta:
Russian Cabbage Soup

Serves 6

Some people confuse this cabbage soup with the cold beet borscht, but this Russian borscht, which we called *capoosta,* is made with beets, cabbage (capoosta), meat and other stuff. Some snobbish Jewish friends won't even acknowledge cold beet soup as borscht, and only accept this Russian kind.

My Russian father loved borscht, hot *or* cold—any way my mother decided to make it. He thought her versions were the greatest.

But don't give me an argument if your mother used more beets, a beaten egg, or whatever. We're entitled to our own tastes, right?

2 pounds beef chuck or brisket, cut in 1 1/2-inch cubes	1 small sweet potato, peeled and sliced
1 onion, sliced	1 large beet, peeled and shredded
2 quarts water	1 large tomato, peeled and cut up
1/2 head red cabbage, shredded	2 tablespoons lemon juice
1 marrow bone	1 tablespoon vinegar
1 carrot, diced	1 tablespoon brown sugar
1 stalk celery, cut in 1-inch pieces	1 teaspoon salt
	1/2 cup raisins

Cook meat and onion in 2 quarts of water over medium heat for 1 hour or until the meat is almost tender. Add cabbage, marrow bone, carrot, celery, sweet potato, beet, tomato, lemon juice, vinegar, brown sugar, salt and raisins and simmer until all the ingredients are tender, but not mushy. If soup is too thick, add a little water. Adjust seasonings to taste.

Schav

Serves 6

Schav is sorrel or sour grass, but it's been years since I've seen the authentic tender little leaves and really sour tasting greens.

Pretty good substitutes are spinach, or fresh beet tops. But then you will have to adjust the flavoring. Taste the leaves first, then decide how much more of this or that you would like. Too much lemon at once could ruin the whole dish, so start with a little and work up. The flavor of schav is similar to that of cold borscht.

On a hot summer day, it's very refreshing, relaxing and also healthful.

1 pound sorrel, spinach, beet tops or other greens
4 cups water
2 tablespoons lemon juice
2 teaspoons sugar
Salt, optional
6 heaping tablespoons sour cream, divided, for serving

3 hard-boiled extra-large eggs, coarsely chopped or sliced lengthwise
Chopped cucumber, for garnish

Cut up greens into little pieces and simmer in water for about 15 minutes or until tender. Add lemon juice and sugar. If you like, add a little salt, carefully. Adjust seasonings and chill.

Serve with a heaping tablespoon of sour cream and 1/2 of a hard-boiled egg, left whole or chopped. I also like to add some chopped up cucumbers.

Russian Cherry Soup

Serves 6

Don't bother with this soup unless you have beautiful plump cherries in season. If you don't, the taste will be *feh*—as Mom would say. You can use any wine you like, but if it's too heavy, you lose some cherry flavor.

1 tablespoon cornstarch	1 inch of a thin stick of
2 cups water	cinnamon
1 pound cherries (about	1 teaspoon sugar
3 cups, pitted)	2 tablespoons lemon juice
1 cup light rose wine	1 cup whipped cream

Make a paste with the cornstarch and 1 tablespoon of the water, then add the rest of the water and stir until smooth.

Set aside 6 of your prettiest cherries. Then, in a food processor or blender, puree the rest to mush. Add the wine, cinnamon, sugar and lemon juice. Cook over medium heat for about 15 minutes, stirring often. Adjust the flavor by adding more sugar or lemon juice to your taste.

Chill and serve with whipped cream, topped with a cherry.

Fish

"Fiss" was what my mother called fish, which caused great hilarity among her non-Lithuanian friends. But they never made fun of her food. And she served fiss often.

Fish is plentiful on Jewish tables, partly because of the many religious dietary restrictions on meat. It's also pareve, which means it can be used with both milk and meat products.

My aunt Lily agreed with those who claimed it as a brain food and as the reason Jews are so smart. She ate "fiss" every day and was a living recommendation for her theories.

Mom favored pike, whitefish and carp, but would buy whatever the fishman said was best that day: flounder, bluefish, bass or halibut among the many choices. She had favorite flavors, but to me they were pretty much the same—flat—unless perked up with some of these terrific recipes.

Sauteed Salmon

Serves 6

To make this simple, lovely recipe work, the salmon must be fresh and of good quality.

2 tablespoons vegetable oil	3 pounds salmon steak slices
2 tablespoons unsalted butter	2 tablespoons water
1/4 cup lemon juice	Lemon wedges for garnish
2 tablespoons grated onion	Brown Butter Sauce,

Combine oil, butter, lemon juice and onion and mix well. Place salmon in the bowl and turn it several times to coat it with the marinade. Refrigerate for at least 30 minutes.

Transfer salmon to a frying pan and saute over medium heat for about 3 minutes on each side (or longer, depending on thickness) until golden brown and just cooked through. If you like it moist, add 2 tablespoons of water to the pan, cover and cook for a couple of minutes.

Serve with wedges of lemon and a sauce of browned butter. You can go a step further and make a design with thin strips of anchovies and pimentos.

Sweet and Sour Cold Salmon

Serves 6

For this treasure of a recipe, the salmon doesn't have to be fresh, but, of course, fresh is always better. Frozen salmon should be thawed before preparing. Like Mom, I always keep some of this dish in a covered casserole when there is a possibility of drop-in visitors.

About 1 1/2 pounds salmon
  fillets, thick ones
1 medium onion, sliced
2 cups water, or more as
  needed
1/4 teaspoon, plus 1/2 teaspoon
  salt, or more as needed
Pinch of pepper

2 bay leaves
1 teaspoon, plus 2 teaspoons
  sugar, or more as needed
2 extra-large egg yolks, lightly
  beaten
2 tablespoons sour cream
2 tablespoons lemon juice, or
  more as needed

Place the salmon and onion in a large saucepan and cover them with 2 cups of water or more if needed. Add 1/4 teaspoon of the salt, a pinch of pepper, the bay leaves and 1 teaspoon of the sugar and bring to a simmer. Cook for 30 minutes. Remove the pot from the heat and let it cool.

With a slotted spoon, remove salmon from the pot, transfer to a casserole or shallow bowl and set it aside. With the same spoon, remove onion; be sure to reserve the cooking liquid.

Break fish into chunks and arrange them in a casserole.

Strain cooking liquid into a bowl. In another bowl, beat yolks, sour cream, lemon juice, the remaining 2 teaspoons of sugar and 1/2 teaspoon of salt to the liquid. Add this mixture to the cooking liquid. Taste and adjust flavors; add more salt if needed. Pour the resulting sauce over the salmon chunks and refrigerate for at least 24 hours, turning once.

Whole Baked Stuffed Fish

Serves 6

For family and intimate friends you can use small fish such as trout, one per person. But for a gorgeous spread, a whole big fish is very festive, surrounded by vegetables in a pretty design. But always use a fresh one. To be sure your fish is really fresh, try to find a kosher market, as dietary law requires utmost freshness. If you can't, buy your fish in any market you trust.

One day, I was shopping in a kosher market and had the following adventure. The brusqueness of Jewish vendors is legendary; it's often the subject of jokes and stories—which, unfortunately, are sometimes true. I got a brusque one that day when I asked for a whole fish for a party. He cut off the head and I objected and said I wanted it whole—head and all. He got annoyed, but went back to look for it, and returned with a head half the size of my fish's head. He refused to look again for the head that fit. As he was about to lose his temper, I asked him sweetly for a recipe. His mood changed abruptly, and with parental warmth he expounded on the delectable methods of using his fish.

"What about the head?" I asked discreetly.

"Oh, that's nothing—you'll put some 'possley' around it and nobody will know," he said, stuffing a big bunch of parsley into my bag.

The lopsided fish was the hit of the party. But I used Mom's recipe.

Note: Remember that the stuffing needs to stand for an hour or more, so leave yourself enough time.

1 whole big (6-pound) fish, or 6 whole small (1-pound) fish	4 cups Sweet and Savory Challah Stuffing

Preheat the oven to 500°.

Clean fish and dry it well. Rub it inside and out with salt. Stuff and skewer the openings.

Place a sheet of aluminum foil on a baking sheet, carefully place stuffed fish on top and turn up the edges of the foil around it.

Bake for 15 minutes or until browned. Reduce the heat to 425° and bake for about 15 minutes longer or until just done.

Sweet and Savory Challah Stuffing:

1/3 cup (3/4 of a bar) unsalted butter, melted	2 tablespoons honey
4 cups torn up challah or egg bread	1 tablespoon lemon juice
1/2 cup finely chopped celery	1 teaspoon salt, or more as needed
2 tablespoons chopped onion	Pepper to taste
1 cup milk, or more as needed	1/4 teaspoon ground ginger
1 extra-large egg, beaten	2 teaspoons minced fresh parsley

In a large frying pan, heat butter over medium-low heat, being careful not to let it burn. Add celery and onion and cook for about 5 minutes, until they are soft but not brown. Remove from the heat and cool.

Combine all ingredients, mix well, and refrigerate for 1 hour or longer. Bring to room temperature. Adjust the seasonings and add more milk or more bread if needed to give the stuffing a soft texture. Taste and adjust the seasoning again.

Pickled Fish

Serves 6

Everyone seems to like fish this way. It has a mouthwatering bite. With thick slices of fresh pumpernickel and sweet butter or big soda crackers, it's a snappy addition to a big dinner, or a meal in itself. If you can't find a good pickling spice, make your own.

Note: *Be sure to use a heavier fish that won't break apart, such as pike, carp, whitefish or a combination.*

3 pounds fresh fish, cut into chunks	1/2 teaspoon ground ginger
2 large onions, thinly sliced	1/2 cup wine vinegar
1 teaspoon salt	2 teaspoons sugar
1/4 teaspoon pepper	1 tablespoon lemon juice
1 tablespoon Pickling Spice	1/2 lemon, thinly sliced
	1/2 cup water

In a large saucepan, combine fish, 1 sliced onion, salt, pepper, pickling spice, ginger, vinegar, sugar, lemon juice, lemon and water. Bring to a simmer and cook for about 30 minutes.

About halfway through the cooking, taste and adjust the seasoning—the flavor will vary with the flavor of the fish, the spices you use and your own preference. When fish is cooked, remove the pot from the heat and chill.

Arrange the fish on a serving platter, garnished with the remaining sliced raw onion. Decorate with fresh parsley.

Homemade Pickling Spice:

4 bay leaves
1 teaspoon peppercorns
1 teaspoon allspice berries

1/2 teaspoon garlic powder
1/2 teaspoon celery seeds

Combine all ingredients and mix well.

Fish Lotkes

Makes 12 lotkes

If you like to invent, all kinds of things can be added to lotkes: ground carrots or mashed potatoes, or sauces such as tomato, cheese, or a nice cream sauce. So create.

1 pound fish fillets
1 large onion
2 tablespoons dried parsley
4 extra-large eggs, beaten
2 teaspoons sugar
1 teaspoon salt

1/4 teaspoon pepper
1/2 cup milk
1/2 cup matzo meal or more
   as needed
Enough vegetable oil for
   frying

Place fish in a steamer or double boiler and steam over medium heat for about 3 minutes, until opaque and slightly resistant to the touch. Remove from the heat and remove any large bones.

By hand, coarsely chop fish, onion and parsley. Transfer to a large bowl and add egg, sugar, salt, pepper, milk and matzo meal.

Form fish batter into patties. If the batter is too runny, add more matzo meal.

In a large frying pan, heat oil over medium heat. When it sizzles, carefully place patties in the pan, in batches if necessary, and fry for 3 minutes on each side, until they are brown and crisp. Drain on paper towels. Add more oil for frying remaining batches if necessary.

Gefilte Fish

Serves 6 to 8

The classic way to make this delicacy is from a mixture of fresh carp, whitefish and pike, with the dumplings rewrapped in the skins. Cod, trout or pickerel can also be used. Whichever you choose, buy your fish at a fish market, have it filleted there and ask for the head, skin and bones; they make the jelly.

When it comes time to cook, be sure to make a tiny sample dumpling and taste it to adjust the seasoning before cooking the whole batter.

3 pounds fish, scaled and
   filleted, with the head,
   skin and bones reserved
1 large whole onion, plus 3
   sliced onions
1 1/2 teaspoons salt, or more
   as needed
Pepper

1 teaspoon sugar, or more as
   needed
3 extra-large eggs, well beaten
1/4 cup water, plus 6 cups
   water or more as needed
1/4 cup matzo meal
3 carrots, sliced
Horseradish

Using a food processor, grinder or hand chopper, coarsely chop fish fillets with the whole onion. Add salt, pepper, sugar, eggs, 1/4 cup of the water and matzo meal.

Simmer a small saucepan of water. Make a tiny ball and cook it for 10 minutes before shaping the gefilte fish dumplings. Taste the test ball and adjust the seasonings if necessary. When you're satisfied with your test, shape fish batter into balls the size and shape of medium baked potatoes.

Cut fish skins in 2-inch strips, wrap them around the dumplings and secure with toothpicks.

Wrap fish head and bones in cheesecloth and put them in the bottom of a big, heavy pot. Top them with a thick layer of sliced carrots and 2 of the sliced onions. Then, carefully place the dumplings on top. Cover with the remaining 6 cups of water, or more if needed, and let simmer for 1 1/2 hours, adding water if needed.

Remove the pot from the heat, let it cool, and using a slotted spoon, remove the dumplings, tranfser them to a plate and refrigerate.

Strain the cooking liquid into a large bowl. Reserve the carrots and discard the cooked onion, fish head and bones. There should be 1 1/2 to 2 cups of liquid; if there's more, return the strained liquid to the heat in a small saucepan and cook until it reduces in volume. Remove from the heat and chill the liquid until it becomes a soft jelly.

Serve the gefilte fish cold surrounded by the jelly and the cooked carrot slices. Surround it with the remaining raw sliced onion, if you wish. Serve with horseradish.

Note: *The flavor will depend on the combination of fish you use and on your preference in seasonings. Some like it mild, some, more spicy, and some, sweeter. Fool around, using your favorite flavors such as tarragon, ginger, nutmeg, lemon or parsley.*

Fish in Vegetable Sauce

Serves 6

The sauce for this savory dish can be made in large batches and used for many things: by itself as a side dish, or to flavor chicken or meat, or even to make a soup, with potatoes or rice if you wish.

1 1/2 tablespoons, plus 1 1/2 tablespoons vegetable oil, divided

1 1/2 tablespoons, plus 1 1/2 tablespoons unsalted butter, divided

1/2 cup chopped celery

1/2 cup chopped green bell pepper

1/2 cup chopped onion

4 tomatoes, peeled and chopped, or 16 ounces canned tomatoes, drained

1 small clove garlic, minced

1 penny-sized piece of fresh ginger root, minced, optional

3 tablespoons flour

3 cups water

2 pounds fresh carp, whitefish, cod or haddock fillets, cut in small pieces

In a large frying pan, heat 1 1/2 tablespoons of the oil and 1 1/2 tablespoons of the butter over medium heat. Add celery, pepper, onion, tomatoes, garlic and, if you wish, the ginger, and saute for 5 minutes until almost tender. Remove them from the pan with a slotted spoon, transfer to a dish and set aside.

Combine flour and remaining oil and butter in the frying pan, stir and let the mixture bubble for 2 or 3 minutes. Add the water slowly and simmer until thickened. Return the rest of the ingredients to the pan and simmer a few minutes longer.

Add fish last and simmer until it is tender, depending on its thickness, until it is just done. If the sauce gets too thick, just add more water, slowly.

Tuna Salad

Serves 6

There's nothing like a can of tuna with something nice in it when you have to throw a meal together in a hurry. Here is a very special-tasting mixture, and the ingredients are usually on hand.

4 (7-ounce) cans tuna	1 cup mayonnaise
1 stalk celery, finely chopped	Salt
3 medium sour pickles, minced, or 1/2 cup pickle relish	Pinch of garlic powder
	6 to 8 tablespoons lemon juice
1 cup slivered almonds	2 to 3 scallions, minced
4 ounces canned mushrooms, or 1/2 cup fresh, thinly sliced mushrooms	Pineapple slices, cut in half
	Tomato slices, cut in half
	Cucumber slices, cut in half

Combine tuna, celery, sour pickles or pickle relish, almonds, mushrooms, mayonnaise, salt, garlic powder, lemon juice and scallions in a large bowl and mix well.

Using an ice cream scoop or large spoon, place a generous scoop of tuna on each plate and surround each scoop with pineapple, tomato and cucumber slices or whatever you wish.

Breaded Smelts

Serves 6

Be careful with the very small smelts, as they are quite delicate and become messy if not handled gently.

2 pounds smelts	2 extra-large eggs, well beaten
3/4 cup flour	Enough vegetable oil for frying
Pinch of garlic powder	Lemon wedges
1/2 teaspoon salt	

Dry smelts well.

Combine flour, garlic powder and salt in a shallow bowl. Pour beaten eggs into another bowl.

Pour oil into a large frying pan so that it reaches a depth of 1/2 inch. Heat over medium heat, being careful that it does not burn while you bread the fish.

Dip smelts into the flour mixture, coat both sides and pat to remove any excess. Then dip smelts into the egg.

Place breaded smelts into the frying pan and fry for 3 to 4 minutes, until golden brown; turn the bigger ones so they brown on both sides. Remove browned smelts from the pan with a spatula. Drain on paper towels and serve with lemon wedges.

Poultry

I can't remember ever opening Mom's refrigerator
without seeing a chicken. There was always chicken
soup; therefore, that pale boiled chicken was always
there, too, waiting to become a cutlet, a member of a
stew, a salad or just a sandwich. I grew to like it,
denuded and all. The taste was savory, having been
boiled in all that good stuff. I'd sneak a little butter
on a piece of challah or rye, a little ketchup, lettuce,
and pile on the slices of boiled chicken. Then I'd
slowly munch away on a stack of these while I stud-
ied for exams. I'm convinced that the good feeling
and energy I got helped me get good grades.

Fancy recipes for chicken were usually for company or when Mom got into a creative mood.

Roast Capon with Raisin and Almond Stuffing

Serves 6

Raisins and almonds are a typical Jewish *nosh,* and, as I mentioned in the chapter on appetizers, there is even a much-loved lullaby of the same name. So it seemed only natural to develop other goodies with this satisfying combination. Mom's Raisin and Almond Stuffing is one of my favorites.

A mean thing is done to a rooster to make a capon, but it does make him tender. If you can't find a capon, get a tender, fat chicken.

6-pound capon	About 4 cups Raisin and
Salt	Almond Stuffing
	Vegetable shortening

Prepare stuffing. Preheat the oven to 325°.

Rub inside of capon with salt. Pack stuffing into the cavity and tie it closed.

Rub the outside of capon with fat and place bird into a roasting pan. Roast capon for 2 1/2 hours, or until done, allowing 25 minutes of roasting per pound. Baste capon with its own juices every 15 minutes.

If necessary, brown capon by turning up the heat to 400° for the last 30 minutes. The capon is done when dark meat loses its pink color and a meat thermometer inserted in the thick part of the thigh reads 180° to 185°.

Raisin and Almond Stuffing:

1/2 cup minced onion	2 extra-large eggs, beaten
1/3 cup vegetable shortening	3 cups cooked brown rice
1/2 cup raisins	1 teaspoon salt
1/4 cup chopped slivered	Pinch of pepper
almonds or ground almonds	Pinch of grated nutmeg

Saute onion in fat until golden brown.

Meanwhile, in a mixing bowl, combine the rest and mix well. Transfer to the pan with onions, stir and saute for a few minutes, until mixed well.

If stuffing is too thick, add a little water to make it thinner.

Boiled Soup Chicken, Fixed Up

Serves 6

The chicken left over from soup is nice all by itself. After all, it was cooked with seasonings and vegetables. But if you want to snap it up a little, here's a wonderful method.

1/4 cup chicken fat	1 clove garlic, crushed
Matzo meal or matzo cake meal for breading	Salt and pepper, optional
	Vegetable of your choice
1 boiled chicken, cut up	About 1/2 cup wine or sweet sherry
2 onions, sliced	

Preheat the oven to 400°.

Place chicken fat into a dish. Pour matzo meal into another dish.

Roll chicken pieces in fat, and then in matzo meal to coat.

Place chicken in a casserole and surround it with onions and garlic. Season with salt and pepper if you wish. If you like, you can add vegetable of your choice, cut up, for a one-dish meal.

Baste chicken with wine and bake, allowing 25 minutes per pound. Baste with pan juices every 15 minutes, until chicken is golden brown and the dark meat loses its pink color.

Roast Turkey with Anna's Stuffing

Serves 10 to 12

A childhood chum of Mom's made great turkey stuffing, but she couldn't give us a recipe. She just threw in whatever came to mind or what she had in the house. Fortunately, the day we watched her make it one Thanksgiving, the result was luscious.

I don't have to tell you, a turkey is one of the best ways to feed a crowd.

10- to 12-pound turkey, or
  1 pound per person
Lemon wedges
Salt

3 to 31/2 cups Anna's Stuffing
1/2 cup sweet white wine, for
  basting

Prepare the stuffing.

Preheat the oven to 325°. Rub inside of turkey with lemon wedges and sprinkle with salt. Lightly pack stuffing into neck and body cavities. Place turkey into a roasting pan, belly up, and baste with wine.

Roast for 3 1/4 to 4 hours, or allow 20 minutes per pound. Baste every 15 minutes with pan juices.

Halfway through roasting, turn turkey over and continue to roast until it browns. Then cover the top with foil and continue to roast, if necessary. The turkey is done when a meat thermometer inserted in the thick part of the thigh reads 180° to 185°.

Anna's Stuffing:

1 cup bread crumbs or
  1/2 small challah
1/2 cup rolled oats
1 cup corn flakes
1/2 cup matzo meal
1/2 cup flour
1 onion
Salt and pepper
2 teaspoons sugar

1 clove garlic, mashed
2 apples, cored, peeled and
  chopped
1/2 cup coarsely chopped
  walnuts or chestnuts
Fat from the turkey, cut up,
  about 1/4 cup
3/4 cup chicken broth

In a large bowl, combine bread crumbs or challah with oats, corn flakes, matzo meal, flour, onion, salt, pepper, sugar, garlic, apples, nuts and turkey fat and mix well. Add enough broth to make the stuffing soft and thick. Taste and adjust the seasonings.

Chicken Giblet Fricassee

When I asked her for this recipe, Mom had no recollection of ever having made it, though we had it once a week when I was little, and it was my favorite dish. What happened is that she had blocked it out because she had only used it during the family's lean years, using leftovers, giblets, chicken feet, backbone, neck and whatever else was inexpensive. Picking out the teensy bits of meat from those little necks and bones and sucking and chewing on them was sheer delight to me. I didn't know it was next to a tragedy to her, being reduced to economize to that degree. Now and then, tiny meatballs were added, the size of marbles. I thought they were adorable.

Mom wouldn't make this dish after she didn't need to, thinking it made her look chintzy, but I added this delicacy to my repertory.

Note: For this dish, you can start with the parts that come with a whole chicken and buy extras from your butcher, feet and all.

About 8 cups of chicken parts and giblets (wings, neck, liver, heart, stomach, feet)
2 carrots, sliced
4 stalks celery, sliced
2 tablespoons chicken fat
2 large onions, finely chopped
1 green bell pepper, chopped
2 tomatoes, cut in small chunks
1 tablespoon flour
2 teaspoons salt, or more or less as needed
Little Meatballs

Place chicken, carrots and celery in a big pot, cover with water and cook over medium heat for about 20 minutes, until the chicken is just done, but not too soft. Reduce the heat to low and ladle out 2 cups of the broth.

Heat chicken fat over low heat. Add onions and green pepper and saute for 10 to 12 minutes, until vegetables are golden brown.

Make a thickener of flour and a little of the broth, adding more broth until you have a smooth paste.

Add onions, green peppers and flour mixture to the pot containing chicken and vegetables, bring it to a simmer and gently place little meatballs on the top. Simmer for about 15 minutes, until meatballs are cooked through.

Little Meatballs:

1 cup chopped meat
1/4 cup mashed potatoes
1 teaspoon salt

1/8 teaspoon pepper
1 small onion, grated
1 extra-large egg

In a mixing bowl, combine chopped meat, mashed potatoes, salt, pepper, onion and egg yolk. Mix well. Make into little balls the size of Concord grapes.

Baked Chicken Sadie

Serves 6

Nothing could be simpler, and a savory baked chicken was a Sadie specialty, put together in a jiffy. It's tasty enough for the finest company dinner. With a fancy rice pudding and a colorful salad, it's a meal fit for any V.I.P.—which includes those you love.

Prepared corn flake crumbs are okay if you can find them, but regular corn flakes crushed with a rolling pin are better.

1 1/2 cups crushed corn flakes
or prepared corn flake
crumbs
2 teaspoons Lawry's seasoned
salt
2 teaspoons salt
1/2 teaspoon garlic powder

1/2 cup vegetable oil or melted
shortening
4-pound chicken cut up
(wings, drumsticks, thighs
and half-breasts), dried well
1/2 cup chicken broth or
water

Preheat the oven to 400°.

In a plate, combine crumbs with seasoned salt, salt and garlic powder and mix well. Pour oil into a shallow bowl.

Roll chicken first in oil, then in corn flakes.

Place chicken in a baking pan and add 1/2 cup broth or water.

Bake for 1 hour, or until done. The chicken is done when the dark meat loses its pink color and a meat thermometer inserted in the thick part of the thigh reads 180° to 185°.

Roast Duck
with Peach Stuffing

Serves 6

Roasting a duck is a little tricky because ducks have a lot of fat, which must be melted slowly. First, your duck must be a fresh, tender bird; otherwise, it can be tough and rubbery. Next, it should be cooked for a long time at low heat to allow the fat to slowly drip away. A V-shaped rack placed in a dry, flat pan (don't add water) is the best roasting container. Lots of attention and basting will give you a crisp, delicious treat. As for the stuffing, start with tasty bread crumbs, homemade if possible.

5-pound duck (or duckling if
   you can find one)
1 1/2 cups Peach Stuffing

1 cup grapefruit juice
1 cup white wine

Prepare the stuffing.

With a fork, make deep pricks all over duck. Pack stuffing into the cavity, and place duck on a V-shaped rack in a dry baking pan and place the pan into a cold oven. (This helps the fat melt slowly.)

Roast at 325° for 1 3/4 hours, or about 20 minutes per pound. Baste duck with some of the grapefruit juice and wine and continue basting with wine and juice every 15 minutes. If necessary, increase the temperature to 425° for the last 15 minutes to brown.

Peach Stuffing:

1 cup bread crumbs
1/2 cup crushed canned
   peaches
1/4 cup chopped walnuts

Giblets and cut-up fat from
   duck, in very small pieces,
   precooked
1 cup chicken broth

In a large bowl, combine bread crumbs, peaches, walnuts, giblets and fat. Add broth a little at a time, until the mixture is moist and soft.

Chicken Shtiklach

Believe it or not, Mom fell in love with a Chinese dish: batter-fried chicken pieces and Chinese vegetables. She even gave them a Yiddish name: *shtiklach*. Ordinarily she didn't trust Chinese food, convinced that lard was lurking in the sauces. Our friend, Kim Chan, of the old House of Chan Restaurant in New York City, won her trust and got her to eat some by personally supervising the cooking.

Making shtiklach, though, was as far as she would go in her own home. She served them with vegetables that she knew, and rice on the side. If you want to go all the way, get a prepared sweet and sour sauce and mix shtiklach and sauce together with Chinese vegetables.

3 chicken breasts, skinned, boned and cut into small pieces
1 1/2 cups flour
1 1/2 teaspoons baking powder
1 1/2 teaspoons salt
3 extra-large eggs
1 1/2 cups water
1/4 cup plus 2 tablespoons vegetable oil

Combine flour, baking powder and salt in a large bowl. In another bowl, beat eggs, add water and oil and mix to combine. Add this mixture to dry ingredients and mix well. If resulting batter is too thick, add a little more water.

Dip chicken pieces in batter, coating them well.

Pour 1/2 inch oil into a frying pan and heat over medium heat. When it begins to sizzle, carefully place chicken pieces into the pan.

Fry for about 2 minutes on each side until golden brown and crispy. Keeping a consistent temperature is crucial, so watch it carefully, adjusting as you go.

Pineapple Chicken Dena

Serves 3

My daughter Dena's favorite dish was always ready for her at Mom's when she visited. It's a bit messy to make, but a big batch stays well in the freezer, ready to heat and eat in 15 minutes.

3-pound chicken	1/2 cup water
2 tablespoons flour	1/2 teaspoon ground ginger
1 teaspoon salt	2 cups (about 16 ounces)
Enough vegetable oil	canned unsweetened
for frying	pineapple chunks, juice
	reserved

Dry chicken well and cut it into small pieces at the joints. Put flour and salt into a paper or plastic bag, add chicken pieces and shake to coat.

In a large frying pan, heat oil over medium heat. When it begins to sizzle, add chicken and cook for about 10 minutes, until browned.

Pour off excess oil, add water and ginger, cover and simmer for 20 minutes. Watch chicken closely to make sure it doesn't stick to the pan; add water if needed. Add pineapple juice and cook for 5 more minutes, then add pineapple chunks and cook for 10 more minutes.

Chicken Pie, a Special Way

Serves 6

When I criticized my mother's first effort at chicken pie because of the soggy bottom, she came up with this ingenious solution. And it's another way to use up the chicken from your homemade chicken soup. For the crust, Mom always used Crisco, but you can use your favorite vegetable shortening.

1 medium onion, chopped
1/2 cup celery, sliced
1/2 cup carrots, sliced
1/2 cup potatoes, cubed
1/2 cup fresh or frozen peas
3 tablespoons shortening
3 tablespoons flour
2 extra-large egg yolks,
  beaten
3 cups chicken broth

1 chicken, skinned and boned,
  boiled with a carrot and
  celery stalk and cut into
  bite-sized pieces
1/2 teaspoon sage
1 tablespoon minced parsley
1 teaspoon salt
Pepper
Pie crust rounds

Cook vegetables, timing them so that they are all cooked tender but not too soft.

In a large saucepan, heat oil or shortening over low heat. Gradually add flour and stir until the mixture sizzles and makes a brown paste. Slowly stir in yolks and broth. Stir quickly and constantly to avoid lumps, until sauce is thick and smooth.

Transfer vegetables to thickened sauce. Add chicken pieces and seasonings and simmer for 30 minutes. Add broth if needed.

To serve, place a few of the round crusts on each platter, spoon some of the chicken mixture over them, and top with a few more crusts. You can serve extra crusts on a plate on the side, wrapped up in a nice linen napkin.

Crust:

Makes about 18 round crusts

2 1/2 cups flour
1 teaspoon salt
3/4 cup plus 2 tablespoons
  shortening

2 tablespoons chicken fat
About 6 tablespoons ice water

Preheat the oven to 450°.

Combine flour and salt. Cut in shortening and chicken fat and mix until well combined and crumbly. Add water, a little at a time, until you can make a ball that does not stick to your fingers.

Then, here's how this recipe is different: Roll out dough on a work surface and cut it into 3-inch rounds. Place rounds on baking sheets and bake for 10 minutes or until light brown and done.

Shikker Chicken

Serves 6

Mom's use of wine was limited to cooking. One sip and she claimed drunkenness and had to go lie down. But she discovered the taste and tenderizing quality of wine with chicken, and one day she decided that if a little is good, more is better. It's also the easiest chicken recipe I know. You can use white wine, but a good sherry is lovely.

1 whole chicken	Pepper
Vegetable oil	Wine
Salt	

Preheat the oven to 350°.

To prepare chicken, leave the big cavity open, but sew up any other openings with heavy thread so that the chicken can sit like a little bowl, just to hold the wine in the cavity. Rub chicken inside and out with oil and season with salt and pepper.

Place chicken in a shallow baking pan so that it stands firmly, propped up on a rack. (Use cooking paper if needed). Pour some water on the bottom of the pan.

Fill the cavity with wine or sherry. Roast for at least 1 hour, until chicken is tender, allowing 25 minutes per pound. The chicken is done when dark leg meat loses its pink color and a meat thermometer inserted in the thick part of the thigh reads 180 to 185°.

Meat

Although meat is subject to many restrictions in Jewish dietary tradition, there is no limitation on the
imagination of Jewish cooks. My mother's only
requirement was that it be well-cooked. I never saw
pink meat until I was grown. She didn't think all the
germs were killed unless meat was cooked at high temperature for at least an hour. Three was more sure.

The exception was lamb. She would let it be pink
for others, but I know she took hers back to the
oven until near charred. So you won't find anything
à point, as the French say, or rare, in this collection
(except the lamb recipe), but you will love these
dishes, and at least you will be sure they are
hospital-sterilized.

Stuffed Flanken

Serves 6

Flank steak is tough, but very tasty. It responds well to slow roasting and ingredients that tenderize it, such as onions.

Note: *Have your butcher cut "pockets" in the steaks. Kosher butchers may think you mean short ribs, which have bones in them. Insist on the boneless flanken.*

2 boneless flank steaks, about 1 1/2 to 2 pounds each, with pockets cut into them	Pepper
	Enough vegetable oil for frying
Flour for dusting	Challah Stuffing
Salt	1/2 cup water

Prepare the stuffing. Preheat the oven to 350°.

Dust steaks with flour, pound to tenderize and season with salt and pepper. Then, in a frying pan, heat oil over high heat. When it sizzles, carefully place the steaks in the pan and cook for about 1 minute on each side, until brown on both sides.

Remove from the heat and transfer to a work surface. Stuff each "pocket" with Challah Stuffing and tie it with string or fasten with skewer. Place in a baking pan, add 1/2 cup water, cover and roast for 1 1/2 to 2 hours, turning once and basting a few times.

Challah Stuffing:

4 cups torn-up challah, softened in water	1/4 cup shortening
1/4 teaspoon sage	1/2 cup finely chopped celery
1/4 teaspoon thyme	1 teaspoon salt
1 cup grated onions	1/4 teaspoon pepper

Combine the challah, sage, thyme, onions, shortening, celery, salt and pepper and mix well. Add a little water to make a soft batter.

Shashlik David

Serves 6

Visions of flaming swords, balalaikas, choral groups and gymnastic dancers spring to mind with the mention of *shashlik*. We never had flaming swords at our house, but my father, David, was a great host and loved parties with music and lots of great food.

Papa, a first class charmer, wheedled this recipe out of a chef in a Russian restaurant.

Shaslik David:

6 pounds leg of lamb cut in
   1 1/2-inch cubes
Marinade
Cherry tomatoes
Pineapple chunks

Mushrooms
Green bell peppers, cut in
   chunks
Small onions

Prepare marinade. Place lamb in a covered container, pour the marinade over it and refrigerate for 1 or 2 days, turning the lamb often.

When you are ready to cook, preheat the broiler.

Spear the lamb on the skewers, alternating it with cherry tomatoes, pineapple chunks, mushrooms, green pepper chunks and small onions. Broil for about 15 minutes or longer, until the meat is done the way you like it. Turn once during the broiling.

Marinade:

3 teaspoons garlic powder
2 tablespoons Italian herbs
   (that's right!). See page 77 to
   improvise Italian seasoning
1 tablespoon instant onions
1 teaspoon salt
1/2 teaspoon sugar

1/2 teaspoon powdered
   mustard
1/2 teaspoon ground ginger
1/2 cup vegetable oil
1/2 cup white vinegar
1/2 teaspoon lemon rind

Mix well.

Cold Roast
Leg of Lamb

Serves 6

While you are making this favorite, you might as well make a real big one, or even two of these. This makes an elegant dinner for guests or to make the family feel special. With a cold roast in the refrigerator all week long, there is always something tempting around for sandwiches or snacks.

To top it off, the cook can stay out of the kitchen. Just put out a big tray of sliced lamb, with fresh or pre-cooked vegetables, some bread, and you can give full attention to the eaters. All that is left to do is to pour the tea and coffee and bring out the cake.

4-pound leg of lamb, boned
  and trimmed
Marrow fat
1 celery heart
1 clove garlic, cut in slivers

1 teaspoon ground ginger
1 teaspoon vegetable oil
1 tablespoon prepared mustard
1 teaspoon salt
About 2 teaspoons flour

Preheat the oven to 375°.

Pound the lamb into a rectangle and roll it around the marrow fat and celery heart. Tie with string placed 2 inches apart. Then, using the tip of a sharp knife, make random slits in the meat and push the slivers of garlic into them.

In a small bowl, combine the ginger, oil, mustard, salt and enough flour to make a paste. Mix well. Rub the paste into the meat. Bake for 30 minutes. Reduce temperature to 300° and continue baking for about 1 1/2 hours, until the meat is done the way you like it. Figure about 30 minutes per pound.

Brisket of Beef, Cooked to Death

Serves 6

This marvelous dish never fails to evoke ohs and aahs, and is as versatile a stew as you'll ever play with. If you want to add vegetables to the stew, do so for the last 30 minutes or so of cooking time.

Flour for dredging, plus 1 tablespoon flour, optional
3 to 4 pounds brisket of beef, cut in 1 1/2-inch cubes
1 medium onion, chopped
2 cloves garlic, mashed, or 1/4 to 1/2 teaspoon garlic powder
1 teaspoon salt
1 tablespoon ground ginger
1/4 teaspoon ground cinnamon
2 bay leaves

2 tablespoons lemon juice
1 cup sweet Concord grape wine (For this dish, we used Manischewitz wine, but you can use any of those sweet wines that elitist wine connoisseurs condemn as yukky)
2 tablespoons honey
2 sprigs of parsley
1 quart water or beef broth

Pour the flour into a dish, dredge meat lightly in the flour and tap it to remove any excess.

Then dump everything into a big pot and cover with 1 quart of water. Simmer, covered, for about 1 hour.

Uncover and continue to simmer for 1 to 2 more hours, until the meat is tender enough to be cut with a fork. (The cooking time will depend on the quality of the meat.) Stir often and add water as needed. Adjust the seasonings halfway through the cooking. The liquid should be almost cooked out when the brisket is done, leaving a nice, sticky stew sauce. Add flour, up to 1 tablespoon, if needed to thicken the sauce.

Choose vegetables you like. We used 3 to 4 medium carrots, 2 potatoes, 1 1/2 cups string beans, cut in small pieces, a pound jar of crab apples and 12 prunes.

Sweet and Sour Tongue: The Crazy Recipe

Serves 6

A friend of my mother's—a man she thought was next to a saint—brought this dish to a pot luck dinner, but wouldn't share the recipe. I didn't have my car that day and he offered to drive me home. He also came on to me.

I tried to change the subject while nudging his hand off my knee—by discussing the recipe. I got it (the recipe, that is), and from then on, kept him at arm's length.

Mom thought his secrecy about the recipe strange, but chalked it up to the weird ingredients and named it The Crazy Recipe. I never snitched on her 'friend,' so she never knew just how strange he was.

This recipe sounds awful, but when done, it's delicious, and no one can figure out what is in it.

1 fresh tongue, about 3 pounds
2 medium onions, quartered
1 bay leaf
2 stalks celery, cut in pieces
1 carrot, diced
1 teaspoon salt
1 cup cooking liquid from tongue

10 ounces or 1 cup grape jelly—we used Welch's grape jelly
6 ounces or 1/2 cup mustard— we used French's mustard
1 cup raisins

Place tongue in a pot with the onion, bay leaf, celery, carrot and salt. Add enough water to cover. Cover and simmer for 1 hour. Cool until tongue is ready to be handled. Reserve cooking liquid. Peel and slice tongue into 1/2-inch pieces.

Preheat the oven to 350°.

Mix well or blend cooking liquid with jelly and mustard. Pour into a casserole, add tongue and raisins and cover. Bake for 2 hours. Uncover casserole during the last 30 minutes of cooking if you like it brown and crisp on top.

Corned Beef and Vegetable Chunks

Serves 6

We persuaded Mom to eat some corned beef and cabbage at an Irish restaurant famous for this dish. She was generally suspicious of restaurants except Jewish ones, but she accepted this dish. Corned beef to her was Jewish and she insisted that the Irish copied it from us.

After that, she made it at home, adding her own touches.

4 pounds corned beef, uncooked and unsliced

1 head cabbage, cut into 6 wedges

6 medium carrots, peeled and left whole

6 medium potatoes, cut in big chunks

1/2 pound string beans, left whole

Place corned beef in a big pot and cover with water. Bring to a boil and simmer for 30 minutes. Drain, cover with water again and simmer for about 2 to 2 1/2 hours until tender. Transfer the corned beef to a work surface and cut it into 6 chunks.

In a separate pot, steam vegetables about 30 minutes before corned beef is done.

Divide corned beef and vegetables evenly between 6 serving platters and serve piping hot.

Cassie's Favorite Meat Loaf

Serves 6

I think Mom was fond of chopped meat because it has to be tortured by grinding and hot-flame cooking in order to be edible in her kitchen. But she did wonderful things with it. There were several meat loaf recipes, and this was my daughter Cassie's favorite.

2 pounds (4 cups) very lean
  chopped meat
2 extra-large eggs, beaten
1 cup crushed corn flakes
1/8 teaspoon pepper

2 teaspoons salt
16-ounce can stewed
  tomatoes, drained well
  and mashed

Preheat the oven to 350°. Lightly grease a 9-inch loaf pan.

Combine all. Then, using your hands, mix well. Pack the meat into the prepared pan and bake for 45 minutes to 1 hour.

Bananas in Meat Blankets

Serves 6

One evening while we were fixing hamburgers for dinner, I told Mom that in an article on nutrition, I read that bananas were very high in potassium, something the body doesn't get enough of in our average diet. So maybe we could try to sneak in a slice of banana in a hamburger and see what happens?

Remember, she was of the "if-a-little-is-good-more-is-better" school of cooking, also applied to the children's health. This is what she came up with.

1 1/2 pounds very lean
  chopped meat
2 extra-large eggs
1/4 cup bread crumbs, or more
  or less as needed

1/4 cup broth, or more as
  needed
1 teaspoon salt
1 teaspoon sugar
Pinch of cayenne
3 bananas, cut in half

Preheat the oven to 350°.

In a mixing bowl, combine all but bananas and mix well.

Divide into 6 equal portions and pack each around a banana half. Place in a baking pan and bake for 20 to 30 minutes or until the meat is done to your taste.

Breast of Veal with Potato Stuffing

Serves 6

Other stuffings like bread, matzo meal or crackers will work, but potato stuffing is the one I remembered. I only had it once (with potato stuffing) outside my mother's kitchen, and that was at another Lithuanian lady's, so maybe it's a specialty.

1 teaspoon salt
1/4 teaspoon pepper
1/2 teaspoon garlic powder
1/2 teaspoon paprika
1/2 teaspoon ground ginger
4-pound breast of veal, with a
   "pocket" cut into it
1/4 cup melted shortening

Potato Stuffing
1 onion, sliced
2 tablespoons diced celery
2 tablespoons diced carrot
2 tablespoons diced tomato
2 teaspoons lemon juice
1 bay leaf
1/4 cup boiling water

Preheat the oven to 400°.

Combine salt, pepper, garlic powder, paprika and ginger and mix well. Rub this mixture inside the "pocket" of the veal breast.

Fill the pocket lightly with the stuffing. Fasten the opening with skewers or sew with heavy thread to close. Rub the outside of the veal breast with melted shortening.

Place the stuffed breast in a baking pan, add onion, celery, carrot, tomato, lemon juice and bay leaf. Add boiling water to the pan, cover, and roast at 400° for 20 minutes. Reduce the temperature to 350° and roast for 1 hour longer or until the meat is tender. Baste every 30 minutes with the pan juices, adding more water if needed. Uncover for the last 20 minutes to brown.

Potato Stuffing:

1 medium onion, grated
1/4 cup chicken fat
3 to 4 medium potatoes,
   peeled, grated and drained
   (1 1/2–2 cups)
1 extra-large egg, beaten

2 teaspoons parsley,
   optional
1/4 cup flour, or more as
   needed
1 teaspoon salt, or more as
   needed

Stew the onion in the fat until golden brown, then add the rest. Add more flour if needed to make a firm batter.

Tsimmis with Meat and Kneidlach

Serves 6

The word *tsimmis* is a dish and also a colloquialism for a big production or a festivity. Mom fussed with it only for company or, with some mild persuasion, as a special treat for us. One day, when we had a pot of tsimmis going, our upstairs neighbor, Sidney Guilaroff (hairdresser to the great MGM movie stars like Joan Crawford) rang our bell. He had not been especially neighborly before.

"I couldn't help asking—what are you cooking? The smell has been tantalizing me all afternoon," he said.

"Tsimmis," I said, relieved that he wasn't complaining about the clatter of pots and pans and loud dialogue (Mom was hard of hearing).

He went crazy. "Oh, my God," he said, "I knew it, I knew it—it smells just like the tsimmis my mother used to make, but she died before I could get the recipe!"

We invited him over later and gave him a bunch of it—and this recipe. He went away wearing the first smile we had seen on him in three years.

1 to 2 pounds chuck or brisket, cut in 1-inch cubes (depends on whether you favor more meat or more vegetables)	1 teaspoon salt
	3 to 6 cups (about 1 to 2 pounds) sliced carrots
1/2 cup chopped onion	2 tablespoons flour
1/2 cup brown sugar	Matzo ballss, page 27, or Potato Dumplings, page 82

Place meat in a big pot and sprinkle onion on top. Cover with cold water, add sugar and salt and cook over medium heat for 1 to

2 hours until the meat is tender. The cooking time will depend on the quality of the meat. Add water if needed during cooking.

Place the carrots in a separate pot, cover with water and cook for about 15 to 20 minutes until they are tender. (Some carrots are tougher than others.)

Once the meat or the carrots have cooked long enough to flavor the cooking liquid, ladle out 1 1/2 cups from either pot. Then, in a small mixing bowl, make a paste of the flour and cooking liquid, adding a little bit of the liquid at a time and stirring until the mixture is smooth and has no lumps. Season with salt and pepper to taste. This is your sauce. Taste and adjust the flavor.

Preheat the oven to 350°. In a casserole, layer the carrots, meat, more carrots and place the dumplings on top. Drizzle the sauce over all.

Bake, covered, for 45 minutes or longer, until all the ingredients are very tender and the dumplings are cooked through and golden brown. Baste and add more water if needed during the cooking. If the tsimmis is not browned, uncover and turn up heat for the last 15 minutes.

Frankfurters with Beans and Sauerkraut

Serves 6

Naturally, you will check carefully to make sure the frankfurters are all beef and kosher. Get nice big juicy ones, one or two per person. Knockwurst is very good, also.

The bean part is an improvement on the canned variety, based on New England style baked beans. But since it is served in Jewish delicatessens, it wasn't altogether foreign to Mom.

This meal was mostly a concession to me and my kids. Anything she didn't put together herself was under suspicion. But if it was kosher, she usually trusted it.

1 large can (2 pounds) baked
   beans in tomato sauce
1 teaspoon powdered mustard
1/2 teaspoon salt
1 teaspoon brown sugar
2 tablespoons molasses
1 teaspoon honey
1 tablespoon dry onion flakes
   soaked in 1 tablespoon
   warm water for 5 minutes

Dash of paprika
2 tablespoons vegetable oil
6 to 12 frankfurters, or
   enough to serve 6 people
1 pound sauerkraut
1/2 teaspoon anise seeds,
   optional

Put beans and their sauce into a pot and add all but franks, sauerkraut, and anise seeds. Heat according to the directions on the can. Taste and adjust the seasoning before serving.

Meanwhile, in a separate pot, cook franks.

In another pot, heat sauerkraut, adding 1/2 teaspoon anise seeds if you wish.

Serve the franks, beans and sauerkraut together on platters, or serve the franks on rolls with the beans and sauerkraut on the side.

Meat and Potato Pie

Serves 6

As I mentioned before, Mom used chopped meat often and did lots of things with it, but I forgot to mention that she bought the meat, inspected it thoroughly, trimmed off the fat and gristle, and ground it herself. She never trusted what they put into prepared chopped meat. Only the best cuts satisfied her, such as round steak or chuck. I must admit it makes a big difference in taste and texture.

1 1/2 pounds lean chopped meat
fat for frying
1 extra-large egg
3 tablespoons plus 2 tablespoons chicken fat, divided
1 cup broth or more as needed
1 teaspoon plus 1/4 teaspoon salt, divided

1/4 teaspoon Lawry's seasoned salt
1/2 cup crushed corn flakes
1 teaspoon minced parsley
4 cups mashed potatoes
1 extra-large egg, well beaten
1 teaspoon sugar

Brown the meat in the fat, stirring to avoid lumps, about 5 minutes.

Preheat the oven to 350°. Lightly grease a 9-inch pie pan. Combine meat, egg, 3 tablespoons of the chicken fat, 1 teaspoon of the salt, 1/4 teaspoon seasoned salt, corn flakes and parsley and mix with your hands.

In another bowl, combine potatoes, beaten egg, 1/4 teaspoon salt, sugar and the remaining 2 tablespoons chicken fat. Remember to taste before cooking and adjust the seasoning.

Spread 1/2 of the potato mixture on the bottom of the prepared pie plate. Top with meat mixture, spreading it evenly. Top meat with the rest of the potato mixture.

Bake for 20 minutes, increase the heat to 450° and bake for 10 minutes, until the pie is browned on top.

Meat Sauce with Noodles

Serves 4 as a main dish

I got this spaghetti sauce from an Italian friend and served it to Mom with noodles. It became a favorite among her girlfriends.

1/4 cup olive oil
3 tablespoons green bell pepper, finely chopped
2 stalks celery, finely chopped
4 ounces canned mushrooms, small pieces
1 large onion, finely chopped
2 pounds (4 cups) chopped meat
1/2 cup bread crumbs
5 to 6 cups broth or water

14- to 16-ounce can tomato sauce
2 tablespoons ketchup
Pinch of cayenne
1 tablespoon plus 2 teaspoons Italian seasoning, or equal parts dried basil, rosemary, thyme, oregano, marjoram, sage and black pepper
1/2 teaspoon salt
2 pounds flat noodles

In a large frying pan, heat oil over medium heat. Add green pepper, celery, mushrooms and onions and saute for 5 to 10 minutes, until they are soft and translucent. Add meat, mashing it with a wooden spoon to separate any clumps. Add bread crumbs, consomme, tomato sauce, ketchup, cayenne, Italian seasoning and salt and simmer very slowly for about 2 hours. Add more water as you go along for a thick but fluid sauce.

Just before you are ready to serve, cook the noodles in boiling water according to the package directions.

Serve the sauce over the hot cooked noodles. This is even better if warmed up the next day.

Vegetables

The vegetable fare at home when I was a kid left much to be desired. Mom's vegetables were over-cooked and unimaginative. But through the years she became intrigued with the great variety of vegetables available in modern markets. Her creative urge overcame her suspicion of anything new, and she eventually mixed the traditional recipes with some bright new ideas.

Vegetarian Tsimmis

Serves 6

The base for our tsimmis is carrots. You will see recipes with or without prunes, dumplings, meat and white or sweet potatoes. This is another one of those dishes that Jewish cooks argue about. But the dominant flavor should be sweet.

We agreed the following combination was our favorite for a vegetarian dinner.

1 pound prunes (2 1/2 cups)	3 tablespoons honey, or more
2 slices lemon	or less as needed
8 medium carrots, peeled and	1 tablespoon flour
sliced (2 1/4 cups)	1 tablespoon unsalted butter
4 medium sweet potatoes,	or vegetable oil
cubed	3/4 to 1 cup water
1 teaspoon salt	Potato dumplings

Prepare the dumplings.

Cook with water and cook prunes with lemon slices until soft, maybe 15 minutes. Remove prunes from pot and set aside. Discard lemon slices.

Cover with water, add salt and cook carrots and potatoes for about 20 minutes, until crisp (not too soft).

Remove carrots and potatoes from pot and set aside. Heat cooking liquid until it reduces to about 1 1/2 cups.

In a frying pan, make a paste with the fat and flour. Simmer until it bubbles, stirring to remove any lumps. Then add the 1 1/2 cups of liquid. Add honey and stir. This is your sauce.

Arrange ingredients in a covered pot, with dumplings on top. Drizzle the sauce over all. Simmer a half hour with the 3/4 to 1 cup water, adding more if needed. Baste once or twice to keep soft and moist.

Potato Dumplings:

Makes 6 or 12—whichever size you want

2 medium potatoes, peeled, grated and drained (about 1 cup)
1 extra-large egg
1 tablespoon chicken fat

1 teaspoon grated onion
1 teaspoon salt
1/4 teaspoon pepper
1/2 cup flour or enough for a firm batter

Mix and refrigerate until ready to make into dumplings and put into pot.

Lima Bean-Tomato Casserole

Serves 6

A friend who shall be nameless invited us to dinner and served a casserole. Mom enjoyed it enough to ask for the recipe. It was a can of beans and a can of stewed tomatoes. This inspired her usual comment of *"Feh!"* (not to our friend's face, but I could see it in her eyes).

At home she duplicated it with fresh foods.

1 pound (about 2 cups) baby lima beans
1/2 medium onion, sliced
2 1/2 cups water
2 large tomatoes, peeled and chopped
1 cup tomato sauce
1/4 cup green bell peppers, chopped

1 teaspoon minced fresh parsley
1/2 cup unsalted butter
1/4 teaspoon rosemary
1 teaspoon salt
1/4 teaspoon cayenne
3/4 cup brown sugar
1/4 cup lemon juice

Soak limas overnight. Drain and discard soaking water.

Cook limas with onion and the 2 1/2 cups water, covered, for about 1 hour, until beans are tender.

Preheat the oven to 300°.

In a casserole, combine rest of ingredients. Cover and bake for 4 or more hours, until beans are very soft. Stir about every half hour. Add boiling water if needed. Uncover for the last 30 minutes to brown.

Honey-Glazed Ginger Carrots

Serves 6

Mom's favorite treat was crystallized ginger. I always kept her supplied. She slipped it into her carrot recipe one day with terrific results. It was all I could do to keep her from slipping it into almost everything else.

4 cups carrots, sliced
2 teaspoons flour
4 tablespoons unsalted butter
1/2 cup water, or more as
   needed

4 tablespoons minced
   crystallized ginger
1/4 cup honey
Ground ginger

Cook carrots until they are almost tender.

In a large saucepan, heat butter over low heat. Gradually add flour and stir until the mixture is smooth.

Add the carrots, water, ginger and honey and simmer for about 5 minutes, covered. Add a little ground ginger if you are a ginger freak.

Stuffed Mushrooms

Serves 6

Mom was suspicious of mushrooms. It wasn't the fear of being poisoned, strangely enough; it was the frilly little gills under the caps that bothered her, as if they were abnormal, unclean growths. She always scraped them out with the tip of a knife, making a mess of the delicate little button ones.

So I insisted on buying the biggest we could find—lovely 2-inch ones, and I rationalized that if she scraped them, there would be more room for stuffing.

We played with recipes and came up with this luscious one.

Note: The final flavor will depend on the flavors of the sherry and cheese that you use.

12 big mushrooms	2 tablespoons sweet sherry
1 tablespoon unsalted butter, melted	1/4 cup dry bread crumbs
	1/4 cup grated Swiss cheese
2 tablespoons grated onion, or 2 tablespoons dried flakes, soaked in 2 tablespoons warm water for 5 minutes	1/2 teaspoon salt
	1 tablespoon lemon juice
	1/2 teaspoon garlic salt
	1 teaspoon minced parsley
1 tablespoon unsalted butter	1 extra-large egg, beaten
1 tablespoon vegetable oil	1/4 cup broth

Preheat the oven to 350°.

Wash and dry mushrooms, then peel them by pulling back outer skin from the inside in small sections. Remove stems, mince and set them aside.

Brush caps with the 1 tablespoon of melted butter and arrange, open side up, in a flat cake or pie tin.

Saute stems with onions, 1 tablespoon butter and oil. Stir until softened and slightly browned. Add sherry and mix well. Remove from heat and add bread crumbs, cheese, salt, lemon juice, garlic salt, parsley, egg and broth. Mix well. Taste and adjust the seasonings.

Carefully spoon the stuffing into the mushroom caps. Bake for 35 to 40 minutes.

Sweet and Sour Beets

Serves 6

Nearly every cuisine has a version of this dish, which is also called pickled, Harvard or marinated beets. The basic method is similar in all versions, but with variations. This excellent one is Mom's invention.

3 large beets, peeled	1 tablespoon vinegar, or more
1 clove garlic, minced	as needed
1 tablespoon brown sugar	1 teaspoon cornstarch
1 tablespoon lemon juice	1 tablespoon unsalted butter

Cook beets in a big pot until crisp. When cool enough to handle, shred, slice or cut in small cubes. Save about 1/4 cup juice.

Add everything else to the juice.

Simmer all with beet pieces until they are tender and well flavored, about 15 to 20 minutes. Taste and adjust, add more water if needed to maintain a light sauce.

Cauliflower with Sesame and Brown Butter Sauce

Serves 6

We used this simple sauce with other vegetables, and it dresses them up enough for the grandest guests.

A friend brought us a whole cauliflower from her garden one day. It was so fresh and pretty that it seemed a shame to tamper with it. So we steamed it whole on a rack in a big soup pot until crisply cooked, and served it whole with the following sauce.

1 whole cauliflowerw	1/2 cup unsalted butter
2 tablespoons sesame seeds	

Toast the seeds in the butter until golden brown, and just drizzle over the vegetable.

Sauteed Mushrooms and Farfel

Serve 6

I got Mom sold on sauteed mushrooms. She thought they seemed drab, so we added scallions. She always cooked too much of everything, so another day she threw in a batch of leftover farfel and voila!—a unique companion to fish.

Enough vegetable oil for frying
Unsalted butter for frying
3 cups fresh whole button
   mushrooms

2 scallions, thinly sliced
1 cup cooked matzo farfel

In a large frying pan, heat equal amounts of oil and butter over medium-low heat. Add mushrooms and scallions and saute for maybe 10 minutes, until golden brown. Combine with hot farfel.

Spicy Stewed Tomatoes

Serves 6

Remember the recipe for Fish in Vegetable Sauce (p. 47)? We told you about a very useful combination of things that would make all kinds of dishes. So here is a vegetable that is served on the side in a little bowl by itself, because it's between a stew and a soup. You eat it with a spoon. If you serve it with meat, use margarine instead of butter. It's something a little different for a change in vegetables, and it has a nice zip to it that everybody likes.

2 tablespoons unsalted butter
1 teaspoon flour
2 cups water
1 medium onion, finely
chopped
1 clove garlic, mashed and
minced

5 to 6 medium tomatoes,
peeled and chopped
1/2 teaspoon salt
Dash of pepper
2 tablespoons finely minced
green bell pepper
1 stalk celery, chopped

Heat butter over low heat. Gradually add flour and stir until the mixture is smooth.

Add water, onion and garlic and stew until they are soft but not brown. Add tomatoes, salt, pepper, green pepper and celery. Stew for about 15 minutes, until vegetables are tender, adding water if necessary, to keep them soft. Taste and adjust the seasoning.

Potatoes, Noodles, Rice and More

This section should really be called "Starch." When we were planning a dinner and decided on a main dish, vegetable and dessert, Mom would say, "So what should we have for a starch?" That meant potatoes, noodles, rice and such. It was often the highlight of the meal and planned around, say, a rice pudding or potato lotkes.

Some sensitive souls don't like the word starch. Don't ask me why. But that doesn't stop them from gobbing up these delicacies like there's no tomorrow.

Fried Sweet Potatoes

Serves 6

I only list this because it's a change from the usual fried white potatoes that everybody knows. When she got bored and I suggested something new and different in food or other adventures, Mom would say, "Well, let it be worse, as long as it's different." That's not the case, though, with fried sweet potatoes. They're really good this way.

5 to 6 medium sweet potatoes,
    baked or cooked
Enough vegetable oil for frying

Unsalted butter for frying
Salt, optional

Cool, then slice and fry potatoes in equal amounts of butter and oil over medium heat. Season with salt if you wish and fry until brown. That's all there is to it.

Poppy Seed Noodles

Serves 6

This is a little nothing of a recipe, but you will be surprised at how good it is, and it looks cute, too. To make it very special, use fresh or homemade noodles.

1 pound broad flat noodles,
    cooked
1/4 cup unsalted butter,
    melted

2 tablespoons poppy seeds
Salt to taste

Toss hot cooked noodles with melted butter, poppy seeds and salt, and serve at once. Lightly sprinkle poppy seeds on top if you like.

"Fenthestic" Rice Pudding

Serves 24

I heard my father inviting a guest one day with the lure, "Sadie made her *fenthestic* rice pudding." Papa's Russian accent often merged with Mom's, in which the 't' and the 'th' are sometimes reversed. Other Russian friends said "fontostic." However you say it, this pudding is absolutely fantastic. I don't know another like it and everybody nudges for the recipe.

Note: The most important thing to remember for this pudding is to use short-grain rice, not the instant or converted kind, but the old-fashioned kind that sticks together. Next, you should know that rice varies in moisture content, so you might have to experiment with the amount of water you use to get the right texture; it should stick together lightly but not be gooey. Once you get it right, then always buy the same brand of rice so you will know how much water to use.

Finally, you can substitute bread crumbs and 1 tablespoon of brown sugar for the Rice Krispies, but that's a second choice.

2 cups raw short-grain rice	1 quart half-and-half (15% cream
4 cups water	8-ounce (1 cup) can crushed pineapple
1 teaspoon salt	
1/4 cup unsalted butter	1 cup raisins
4 extra-large eggs, well beaten	Topping
1/4 cup sugar	

Preheat the oven to 350°. Butter a 9-by-13-inch baking pan.

Cook rice, water and salt over medium heat for about 25 minutes.

Put butter into the rice and let it melt, stirring to combine. Next, add eggs, sugar and half-and-half and mix well. Add pineapple and raisins.

Fold the mixture into the prepared pan.

Spread topping evenly on top of the pudding.

Bake 30 minutes. Remove the pudding from the oven and dot with 24 spots of jam, about 1/2 teaspoon each. Try to space them so that the dots are centered on 24 portions.

Return to oven for another 30 minutes until brown and firm.

For streusel-type topping: mix together rice cereal, butter, nuts and cinnamon.

Topping:

1 cup Rice Krispies
1/4 cup (1/2 bar) unsalted
    butter
1/2 cup chopped walnuts

1/2 teaspoon ground
    cinnamon
1/4 cup raspberry jam

Noodle Pudding

Serves 6

My cousin Mildred shared this delectable recipe with us. Guests often ask about calories, usually while stuffing their faces with it, and we must honestly say, "Forget it."

6 extra-large eggs, separated
1 cup sugar
1/4 cup (1/2 bar) unsalted
    butter, melted
1 pint sour cream
Grated rind of 1 lemon, about
    a round tablespoon

16 ounces crushed pineapple,
    drained dry
8- or 10-ounce package
    medium flat noodles,
    cooked

Preheat the oven to 350°. Butter a 9-by-13-inch glass baking pan. Beat egg whites until stiff but not dry and refrigerate.

In another bowl, beat yolks with sugar, add butter, sour cream, rind and pineapple. Mix thoroughly, then fold in egg whites. Reserve 2 cups of this mixture—this is for the final topping.

Add noodles to the rest of the mixture and mix again. Spoon into the prepared pan, then spread the reserved 2-cup mixture on top. Bake for 1 hour.

Baked Stuffed Matzo Balls

Serves 6

Mom called these *chremslach,* but most cookbooks make those like lotkes or balls, deep-fried, or other shapes and methods.

If you are a matzo ball freak like me, you will acquire a fatal addiction to these. Don't make too many, because they will disappear in ten minutes.

2 cups matzo meal	1/4 cup water
4 extra-large eggs, beaten	3 tablespoons chicken fat
1 1/2 teaspoons salt, or to taste	Unsalted butter, melted
1/2 teaspoon sugar	Paprika, optional
1 cup chicken broth	1/2 cup matzo meal

Prepare stuffing.

Preheat the oven to 400°.

In a bowl, combine matzo meal, eggs, salt, sugar, chicken broth and water. Let stand 30 minutes.

Bring a large pot of water to a simmer.

In a separate bowl, combine ingredients for stuffing.

Using your hands, form the batter into 6 oval balls, with stuffing pressed into the centers.

Gently lower the matzo balls into simmering water and cook for about 15 minutes. With a slotted spoon, transfer the matzo balls to a baking dish. Leave a little water on bottom of pan so they don't get too dry.

Bake for 30 minutes or until brown. Baste these with melted butter. You can sprinkle a little paprika on top if you like. Turn once or twice to brown on all sides.

Stuffing:

1/2 cup chicken fat	1 extra-large egg, beaten
1/4 teaspoon ground cinnamon	1/4 cup finely chopped walnuts or other nuts
2 tablespoons honey	2 tablespoons raisins

Boiled New Potatoes with Parsley and Lots of Butter

Serves 6

Another nothing of a recipe, but so good. Wait for the little new potatoes in season. Buy only very fresh ones. Figure 2 to 3 per person.

I asked Mom what was her secret for the great taste of these and she said "Lots butter." But pure sweet butter, the only kind used in her house.

12 to 15 potatoes
1/4 cup unsalted butter,
  melted

2 tablespoons finely minced
  parsley
Salt and pepper to taste

Bring a large pot of water to a boil, and boil potatoes in their jackets until very tender. Peel and toss with butter and parsley. Salt and pepper to taste. Sprinkle with more parsley to serve.

Potatoes and Goo

Serve 6

This was Mom's name for this what-cha-may-call-it. She didn't know she was simply making a brown sauce or what the French call a brown *roux*.

I ate this all through my grade school years when I came home for lunch, usually schlepping along two or three friends. Mom always had a huge pan of goo and cut up boiled potatoes for us. It was probably the only thing she could afford to feed us at the time. I suspect, though, that she sneaked in a little cream with the milk, but never succeeded in getting me fat.

6 medium potatoes, peeled
    and cut in chunks
1/4 cup unsalted butter

1/4 cup flour
1 quart milk
Salt and pepper to taste

Cook potato chunks in water to cover until soft.

Heat butter over low heat. Gradually add the flour and stir until the mixture sizzles and makes a brown paste. Add the milk very slowly, stirring quickly to avoid lumps and simmer until the sauce is well mixed and quite thick.

Just glop it over the hot chunks of potato.

Fried Kasha
(Buckwheat Groats)

Serves 6

Here's a never-fail dish and one you can play with, too. For example, add bits of leftover chicken or meat, mushrooms, or whatever you have around. It's not only delicious, it's very healthful.

2 extra-large eggs, well beaten
1 cup medium-cut kasha
1 teaspoon salt
1 teaspoon minced onion

1 teaspoon minced parsley
2 tablespoons chicken fat or
    unsalted butter
2 1/4 cups rich chicken broth

In a large bowl, mix with beaten egg the kasha, salt, onion and parsley.

In a 10-inch frying pan, melt the fat or butter, add the mixture and stir until dry and toasted, about 5 minutes.

Boil the broth and add slowly to kasha, stirring to keep it smooth. Cover and simmer 15 minutes. The liquid should be absorbed.

Kasha Varnishkes

Serves 6

As I mentioned, you can ad-lib variations of fried kasha. This combination is a classic and is rarely varied.

1 extra-large egg, beaten well
1 cup medium cut kasha
Salt to taste
1/4 cup chopped mushrooms, optional
2 tablespoons unsalted butter,

plus more for sauteing mushrooms
2 1/4 cups chicken broth
2 cups bowknot noodles, cooked

In a large bowl, mix with beaten egg the kasha and salt.

In a 10-inch frying pan, melt the fat or butter, add the mixture and stir until dry and toasted, about 5 minutes.

Boil the broth and add slowly to kasha, stirring to keep it smooth. Cover and simmer 15 minutes. The liquid should be absorbed.

If you decide to add mushrooms, saute them separately in 2 to 3 tablespoons butter. Toss the kasha and mushroom mixture with the cooked noodles and serve.

Potato Lotkes

Makes 2 dozen lotkes

There's an old Yiddish saying: "Where there are two Jews, there are three rabbis"—(to mediate). We are rugged individualists and to tell the truth, pretty opinionated.

So you will find differences of opinion about practically everything, and this includes lotkes. Some like them soft, others crisp, with or without onions or eggs, cooked and mashed first, or grated raw. Ours have a little of everything.

4 medium potatoes, peeled,
  grated and drained well
  (2 cups)
1 medium onion, grated and
  drained well (6 tablespoons)
1/4 teaspoon baking powder
2 tablespoons potato flour

2 extra-large eggs, well beaten
1 1/2 teaspoons salt
1/4 teaspoon pepper
1/2 teaspoon sugar
Enough vegetable oil for
  frying
1/4 cup matzo cake meal

Combine the potatoes, onion, baking powder, flwour, eggs, salt, pepper and sugar.

In a large frying pan, heat vegetable oil, 1/4-inch deep, until it sizzles. Ladle potato batter into the pan in 2-by-3-inch pancakes. Fry for 2 minutes on each side, until brown and crisp.

Serve with sour cream or applesauce—the traditional way.

Individual Potato Kugelach, Muffin Size

Makes 1 dozen

My kids used to fight for the crisp crust of the regular potato pudding. Mom solved this by baking it muffin-style, which was practically half crust. This makes 12 kugelach, so the children shouldn't fight.

5 to 6 medium potatoes,
  grated and drained (3 cups)
2 extra-large eggs, beaten
1/2 cup grated onion
1/4 cup chicken fat
1 1/2 teaspoons salt

1/4 teaspoon pepper
1/2 teaspoon baking powder
1/3 to 1/2 cup flour, as needed
1/4 teaspoon ground
  cinnamon, optional

Preheat the oven to 375°. Grease a 12-cup muffin tin.

Mix all together and spoon batter into the prepared muffin tin. Bake for about 45 minutes, until crisp and brown. Halfway through, brush the tops of the kugelach with melted butter.

Note: *For very crisp crusts, bake in glass custard cups.*

Homemade Noodles

Serves 6

It's fun to make your own noodles—there is such a difference in taste from store-bought, and as my mother kept pointing out, you know what's in it. Noodles are found in every ethnic cookbook, but recipes vary so much that I didn't find two alike. Basically, the ingredients are flour and liquid. The flour can be white, wheat or otherwise. The liquid can be beaten eggs, water or both. Salt is optional, as is butter or oil. For color and nutrition you can use a puree of spinach, carrots or other vegetables. Herbs can be added, but go easy with these.

The method for making noodles is generally the same; only the width varies. The important thing to remember is to knead your dough well. The amount of liquid you need will vary with the size of the eggs and quality of flour.

Mom's recipe is a sort of in-between one.

2 cups flour	1/2 teaspoon salt
4 yolks or 2 extra-large eggs, lightly beaten	1 tablespoon water, or more as needed

Pour flour into a big bowl or onto a wooden board or other work surface. Make a well in the center and pour in eggs and salt. With your hands, carefully work egg into flour, being careful not to let the egg run. Gradually add water, adding more as needed to make a dough, not too stiff, but not too soft either. Knead with your fingers in a spiral motion, taking in more flour at each turn. When it no longer sticks to your fingers, make into a ball and knead about 10 full minutes until pliable and smooth.

Cover dough with a dish towel and let rest for 30 minutes or so.

Roll out dough into a rectangle as thinly as possible, no thicker than 1/8 inch—thinner if you can. This takes a little muscle action. Roll the dough as you would a jelly roll, then cut through the roll 1/4 to 1/2 inch slices, whatever width you desire. Lay out strips on a cloth. Dry for at least 2 hours and as much as overnight.

Cook as you do regular noodles. They can also be cooked right away—Mom hung them over a towel on the back of a chair until ready.

Knishes

I never saw such a difference of opinion about what is a *knish*. The only agreement is that it's like a bun and has a filling. Some have a bread-type dough around it, or a pie-crust dough, with potatoes or whatever as stuffing. Some stuffings have stuffings. Some potato knishes have no wrapping. The whatevers can be meat, chicken, liver, cheese or kasha.

The kind I remembered and dearly loved was sold in old-fashioned delicatessen stores. These were huge, with a thin crust and lots of mashed potatoes inside, with a tang of onions and moist from chicken fat. We got pieces of waxed paper to hold them with. No dainty morsels, these. A cousin of mine makes them like tiny canapes, which are good, but not my idea of a knish, which is hearty and filling—a true *nosh* that can tide you over until dinner.

Dough:

2 1/4 cups flour, or more as needed
1 teaspoon baking powder
3/4 teaspoon salt
2 extra-large eggs, beaten
1/4 cup vegetable oil plus 2 tablespoons

1/4 cup water plus 2 tablespoons or more
1 extra-large egg yolk diluted with water or vegetable oil for glaze

Put flour, baking powder and salt into a big bowl or onto a wooden board or other work surface. Make a well in the center and pour in eggs, water and oil. With your hands, carefully work egg into flour, being careful not to let the egg and oil run. Knead with your fingers in a spiral motion, taking in more flour at each turn. Add more flour if needed to make a firm dough. When it no longer sticks to your fingers, make into a ball and knead about 10 full minutes until pliable and smooth.

Roll out dough on a lightly floured work surface, as thinly as possible.

Preheat the oven to 350°.

Cut dough into 3-inch squares or circles.

Place a spoonful of either meat or potato stuffing on each, fold like a turnover and pinch edges together.

Brush with diluted yolk for a glaze.

Bake for 15 minutes, increase the temperature to 400° and bake for another 5 minutes, until lightly browned but still soft.

Potato Filling:

1 cup minced onion	1 extra-large egg, beaten
1/4 cup chicken fat	1 1/2 to 2 teaspoons salt
2 cups mashed potatoes	1/4 teaspoon pepper

Saute onions in fat until golden brown. Mix the potatoes with the egg. Add the onions. Add salt and pepper to taste.

Meat Filling:

2 onions, finely chopped	2 extra-large eggs, beaten
1/3 cup chicken fat	Salt and pepper
1 pound ground chuck	

Saute onions in fat until golden brown. Add meat to brown. Combine with eggs and season with salt and pepper. If it seems too crumbly, you can add 1 or 2 tablespoons of matzo meal.

Salads

In my childhood years I seldom ate fresh salads in our house or other friends of Mother's. I have already explained that everything was cooked to "kill the germs." Also, when I was little, supermarkets as we know them now didn't exist, and the little grocery stores in New York City didn't look clean enough for her to trust fresh produce. Even fruit was scrubbed within an inch of its life and soaked in kosher salt. This method, I learned later from a doctor, was and still is, the best way to sterilize it against the really bad germs.

As time went on, we introduced more and more fresh greens and vegetables to create salads, and she finally accepted them as a legitimate part of a meal.

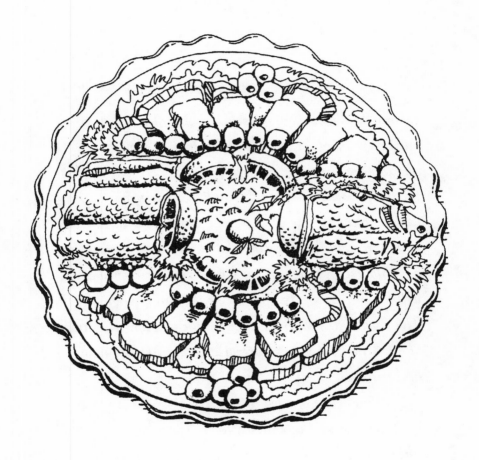

Sour Cream and Minced Vegetables

Serves 6

This is an age-old Jewish dish, one that I ate and relished for many years because it looks like little jewels in a bed of snow.

1 quart sour cream
1/3 cup finely minced radishes
1/3 cup finely minced celery
1/3 cup finely minced carrots
1/3 cup finely minced cucumbers
1/3 cup finely minced green, red or yellow bell peppers
Salt, optional

Simply mix and serve. A little salt may be added.

Lettuce Wedges and Russian Dressing

Serves 6

An ordinary salad is made Jewish by adding herring. You can also use anchovies or make a creation of your own. Non-Kosher cooks have added shrimp, but never in Mom's sight.

1 head iceberg lettuce, tightly packed
3 to 4 tablespoons ketchup, according to taste
3/4 cup mayonnaise
3 to 4 ounces matjes herring, or prepared herring in a jar
About 3 inches of a small dill pickle, sliced

Wash and dry whole lettuce. Cut into 6 wedges. Place each wedge on a salad plate.

Mix ketchup and mayonnaise until smooth, then drizzle it over the lettuce wedge. Top with strips of herring and pickle slices, making your own design.

Carrot and Raisin Salad

Serves 6

This is a favorite dish you will find in most Jewish cookbooks. What makes Mom's different is the trick she used with mayonnaise. She learned it from a French baby nurse I had for two weeks with my first-born. Marie and Mom had coffee klatches, discussing life and recipes.

When you prepare the mayonnaise, be sure you use *only* the yolks.

8 medium carrots
1 cup raisins
1/4 cup water

1/4 cup lemon juice
1 cup French Mayonnaise
Lettuce

Peel carrots and slice 6 nice rounds to use as decoration. Set them aside and shred remaining carrots.

Steam raisins until plump in 1/4 cup water and 1/4 cup lemon juice. Drain and while still warm, toss with carrots and 1 cup of the mayonnaise.

Serve individual salads on bed of lettuce and dollop of the mayonnaise on top. Decorate with carrot slices.

Note: *You can use more or less of the mayonnaise—but it's so good, you can eat it with a spoon.*

French Mayonnaise:

Makes about 2 cups

2 cups mayonnaise
2 extra-large egg yolks
1/8 teaspoon garlic powder

1 tablespoon lemon juice, or
   more as needed

Mix and adjust taste.

Caviar for Peasants

Serves 6

The Russian name for appetizers is *zakuski,* but these are usually hearty dishes that are eaten during the vodka or schnapps drinking. Then, after the guests are happily lubricated, dinner is served. The best known are varieties of cooked cold vegetables. I found this Russian eggplant appetizer so substantial and tasty that I like it as a salad unto itself.

1 medium eggplant
1/2 cup chopped onion
1 green bell pepper, finely
   chopped
1/4 cup vegetable oil
1 large tomato, peeled and
   coarsely chopped
2 tablespoons honey

1/4 teaspoon salt
1/4 cup currants or raisins
1/2 to 1 teaspoon crushed
   garlic
2 to 3 tablespoons lemon juice
   (careful!)
Red lettuce

Preheat the oven to 400°.

Bake eggplant for 45 minutes or until soft through. Peel and chop coarsely.

Brown onions and green pepper in oil. Add the rest and stir for 15 minutes over low heat.

Cool and serve on a bed of red lettuce.

Doris's Spinach Salad

Based on the splendid salad that (I think) originated in California, my good friend and great cook, Doris Siegel shared this Jewish version with us. The non-Kosher version uses crushed bacon.

Note: *Doris used Lawry's packaged De Luxe French Dressing, but if you can't find it, use another you like, oil and vinegar based.*

1 bunch spinach, 8 to 10 ounces	1/3 cup fresh sliced mushrooms
3/4 cup sliced almonds	French dressing—Doris used
About 2 cups very fresh bean	Lawry's dry packaged De
sprouts	Luxe

Preheat the oven to 350°.

Of course the spinach should be washed and dried well and then torn by hand into bite-sized pieces.

Toast the almonds for 10 to 15 minutes, but be careful they don't get too dark—they go quickly.

Toss together just before serving.

Beet-Mandarin Salad

Serves 6

The flavors are a particularly nice blend here, as is the eye appeal of the bright colors. You'll probably use this over and over for all types of meals.

14 to 16 ounces canned	1 bunch watercress
pickled beets, sliced	1 cup mayonnaise
20 ounces canned mandarin	Grated nutmeg
oranges	

Arrange beets and mandarins on greens and top with dollop of mayonnaise. Sprinkle a pinch of nutmeg on top.

Cauliflower Chunks

Serves 6

Once Mom learned to make her special Russian dressing, she didn't quit. One day she was feeling blue, and I needed a break, so we drove out to the country and had lunch in an inn where we were served this sort of relish salad. Finding a nice new recipe cheered us up. We immediately adopted it, adding a few items, and Mom named it Cauliflower Chunks.

1 head cauliflower	1 cucumber
1 bunch radishes	Russian Dressing
3 carrots	

Break cauliflower into small buds or pieces. Clean radishes. Cut carrots and cucumber into sticks.

Combine ketchup and mayonnaise to make dressing and transfer to a pretty bowl.

Arrange vegetables on a platter around the bowl of dressing.

Pierce chunks with large toothpicks. Use the dressing as a dip.

Russian Dressing:

4 to 6 tablespoons ketchup	1 cup plus 2 tablespoons mayonnaise

Beefsteak Tomatoes on Watercress

Serves 6

During World War II my parents kept a "Victory Garden" like many others, and one of their specialties was huge, delicious tomatoes. They were so good, it seemed only respectful to leave them alone, except for a light dressing.

Salad:

3 beefsteak tomatoes

1 bunch watercress

Peel and cut tomatoes in half crosswise. Marinate for 30 minutes in vinaigrette.

Make a tiny slice on the bottom of tomato if needed to stand them up straight and arrange on beds of watercress.

Vinaigrette:

2 tablespoons wine vinegar
1/2 cup safflower or other
 vegetable oil

Salt and pepper

Combine vinegar and oil and season with salt and pepper.

Doll Salad

Serves 6

For several years I shared a duplex with my mother when my daughters were little. She often snooped around to make sure there was enough food, even though my refrigerator was always packed. One day I complained that the girls had stopped eating fresh vegetables, but I didn't have the patience to nag, figuring they would get around to it, and simply continued to offer salad.

"In the old days, we used tricks to get the children to eat," Mom said.

"Be my guest," I said. She came up with this salad—it varied every time, and disappeared from the plates every time, too.

Take a large platter for each little person and make a Raggedy Ann figure or face on it with different combinations, such as:

Hair: Lettuce or carrot curls
Head: Cottage cheese spread in a little circle or fruit halves

Body:	Half apple or pear
Arms & legs:	Cheese sticks, cucumber pieces, celery or bananas

You can also make a big face of cottage cheese or shredded vegetables, with a big banana smile, and eyes of marshmallows, dates or prunes.

Pickled Vegetables

Serves 6

Mom got this recipe from—would you believe?—a Guatemalan cleaning lady she had for a spell. She always served lunch to her helpers and, over coffee, discussed life in other countries, making quite a sociologist out of her.

4 carrots	1/4 of a cabbage
4 beets	3 scallions

Shread carrots and beets, finely chop cabbage and mince scallions. Marinate in dressing. Serve in a glass bowl.

Marinade:

6 tablespoons vegetable oil	1 or more teaspoons salt
1/4 cup wine vinegar	1 or more teaspoons sugar
2 tablespoons lemon juice	1 teaspoon celery salt
1/2 teaspoon dried oregano	

Combine all and let stand at least 2 hours. Taste and adjust flavors.

Noshes
or Snacks

A Jewish nosh is something great to eat, or something to munch on between meals, or a snack instead of a meal. But some of the offerings here can be served with other things or with a big meal.

Russian Egg

Serves 2 kids who are "not hungry"

Another day when my kids were giving me a hard time at breakfast, Mom walked in on us and asked what was wrong.

"They won't eat breakfast," I cried.

While chasing each other around the room, they shouted, "We're not hungry."

I saw the 'tricks' gleam in Mom's eyes as she called to them "How would you like a Russian Egg?'

"Yeah, yeah," they yelled and chased each other into the kitchen.

I whispered to Mom, "What's a Russian Egg?"

"I dunno—I'll think of something," she said with a shrug.

All she did was to take two small fry pans and fried two eggs in each with "lots butter" until the butter was browned. Out came my big wooden pastry board and she served the eggs on the board, still in the pans, bubbling hot.

The little *momsers* not only polished off the eggs, but sopped up the sauce with lots of challah and butter and washed them down with milk—and then—asked for seconds!

They ate Russian Egg for weeks after that, until it was coming out of their—and my—ears. This trick worked for years whenever they were "not hungry."

Scrambled Eggs and Lox

This recipe is typical of a Jewish nosh and can be served at a big breakfast or brunch or any festive occasion.

Enough unsalted butter for
   frying
1 or 2 extra-large eggs per person

Milk or water
Lox

In a large frying pan heat the butter over low heat. Beat eggs and milk. Chop lox and add to egg. Fry in the prepared pan.

Eggs and Salami Semi-Omelette

Enough vegetable oil for frying
Thinly sliced salami
1 or 2 extra-large eggs per
  person

Fried potatoes
Pineapple slices
Tomato, sliced

In a large frying pan heat oil over low heat, add salami and fry until slightly brown. Meanwhile, beat eggs and add to pan. Push eggs around until they are nearly done but not dry, then turn over, omelette style. Serve with fried potatoes, pineapple and tomato slices.

Oatmeal-Nut Pudding

Serves 6

Late one evening, a couple of Mom's friends dropped in after a movie. They caught her without her usual stock of noshes, as we had been working on special recipes.

Out of her bag of tricks, she made one up for adults and asked if they would like a nut pudding. This is what she improvised.

Note: *Steel-cut oats are crunchy and nutty all by themselves. They will take 45 minutes to cook. Rolled oats aren't the same and won't work in this recipe.*

4 cups cooked steel-cut oats
Unsalted butter
Cream

Brown sugar
Chopped walnuts

Serve the oatmeal hot and thick with a big dab of butter in the center, a circle of cream around the rim and sprinkled with brown sugar and lots of chopped walnuts.

Accompany with an assortment of crackers, butter and orange marmalade.

Orange Izzy

Serves 6

Most of you are probably familiar with Orange Julius, a popular drink. I brought one home for a filling snack one afternoon. I never could figure out what was in it except for orange juice. Mom sniffed and tasted it, but didn't approve. She sort of duplicated it, only better. I teased her, warning that she would be sued by the Orange Julius company.

"So we'll call ours Orange Izzy," she said, naming it after a relative we both liked.

1 quart milk
2 cups fresh orange juice

2 extra-large eggs
Honey to taste

Beat or whirl in blender.

Fried Matzo

Serves 6

Fried matzo, also called *matzo brei,* is a snack we make periodically. The taste will vary with the matzo. I like the savory egg-onion kind for that extra flavor. Some like the whole wheat variety. One matzo per person is usually about right.

1 extra-large egg per matzo	1 matzo per person
1 tablespoon milk or water per extra-large egg	"Lots butter" (unsalted) for frying
Salt to taste	

There is really nothing to it. Beat the eggs with milk or water. Season with salt to taste. Break up the matzo into bite-sized pieces and soak in the egg mix for about 15 minutes. Fry in Mom's "lots butter" secret. You'll love it.

Shalta Nozzis

Serves 6

Similar to Lithuanian Hot Dish, this recipe is especially dear to me because of the following event.

The late William Lawrence was for many years the science editor of the *New York Times,* and a greatly honored journalist. I was fortunate to have Bill and Florence, his wife, as friends when I lived in New York. Bill had come here from Lithuania as a boy, without money and not speaking English, and worked his way through Harvard University in the classic immigrant manner.

When my mother planned to visit me, he wanted to meet her, and I arranged a dinner party, inviting a group of celebrities who wanted to meet Bill.

Mom made her best-remembered Old World dishes, including Shalta Nozzis, which means cold noses. Bill went wild over it and also over Mom. He cornered her and they conversed in Lithuanian all evening, neglecting the V.I.P.s.

Dough:

3 1/4 cups flour	3/4 cup milk
3 extra-large eggs	1/4 cup unsalted butter,
1/4 teaspoon salt	melted
1/4 teaspoon sugar	

Mix as for noodle dough, knead smooth, roll thin and cut into 3-inch squares. These are your *kreplach.*

Filling:

1 pound hoop cheese or dry cottage cheese

3 ounces cream cheese

1/4 cup ground nuts

1/4 teaspoon sugar, or more as needed

1/4 teaspoon salt, or more as needed

Mix together well, mashing cheese if necessary.

To assemble:

You'll need one cup sour cream, 1/4 cup butter, and 1/2 cup chopped almonds. A little cinnamon and sugar if desired.

Put a spoon of filling onto dough and press into oblong kreplach or triangular turnover shapes. Lower into gently simmering water for 5 minutes.

Butter a 3-quart casserole and place a layer of kreplach, cover with 3 tablespoons sour cream and dots of butter. Repeat 3 times, topping with sour cream. Sprinkle sugar and cinnamon on top, and press in the almonds.

Bake at 350° uncovered, until brown. If it doesn't brown after 1/2 hour, turn oven to 400°, then back to 300° to finish—altogether 45 minutes. If it gets dry, add water.

Serve cold. I know, I know—it's complicated, but this kind of cooking is an artistic work and develops patience and creativity.

Zucchini Lotkes

Serves 2

I thought Mom invented these as an underhanded way to get more vegetables into me, but I found versions of them in many cookbooks, including Jewish ones. Try other vegetables such as broccoli, but cooked crisp.

4 extra-large eggs, beaten
1 teaspoon minced onion
2 teaspoons lemon juice
1/4 teaspoon salt
1/4 teaspoon grated nutmeg

Pinch of garlic powder,
  optional
1/2 cup shredded zucchini
Oil for frying

Mix everything together and fry in hot oil like pancakes. If you like thicker pancakes, add 2 or more tablespoons matzo meal and let stand 30 minutes before frying.

Helzel
(Stuffed Chicken Neck)

Serves 6

Opinions vary, but my favorite *helzel* tasted the same to me as *kishka*. The stuffing is the same, only helzel is a poultry neck and kishka is beef casing or intestine. If you can survive that image, you can enjoy this *tom*—tasty morsel.

Note: Gribben *are chicken cracklings. See page 163*

3 to 4 casings from chicken
  necks
1/4 cup vegetable oil or
  chicken fat
1/4 cup minced onion
1 teaspoon salt

Pinch of pepper
Pinch of paprika
1/2 cup flour
1/4 cup chicken broth
Gribben, optional

Wash the insides of casings and scrape clean. Sew one end.

In a frying pan, heat oil over medium heat, add onion and stew until golden brown. Let cool a bit and add salt, pepper and paprika. Add flour and mix well. Add broth, a little at a time, to make a soft mix.

Stuff casings 2/3 full and sew up the other ends. Plunge stuffed casings into boiling water enough to cover, and simmer 1 hour.

Transfer to a roasting pan. Roast by themselves or with a chicken 1 hour or longer, turning once or twice until crisp and brown.

Lithuanian Hot Dish

Serves 6

This lovely snack was contributed by a young salesgirl we met in a gift shop, and my daughter's first namesake, Dena Lisovskis. She learned it from her aunt—a true heirloom recipe, since she was a second-generation Lithuanian. This is exactly how she wrote it down for us.

1 pint low-fat, small-curd
  cottage cheese

4 extra-large eggs
2 tablespoons minced chives

Preheat the oven to 325°.
Mix together and put into a buttered baking dish. Bake uncovered for 45 minutes.

Blintzes

Makes 18 to 20 blintzes

I've tasted blintzes made with an almost endless variety of fillings and combinations: chopped liver and potatoes, meats, vegetables, prunes, berries and all kinds of fruits. They are to Jews what crêpes are to the French.

Batter for Blintz Leaves:

2 extra-large eggs
1 cup flour, more as needed
1 cup milk, or more as needed
1 tablespoon unsalted butter,
  melted, or vegetable oil

1/2 teaspoon sugar
1/2 teaspoon salt
Filling

Beat eggs well, add flour, milk, eggs, butter or oil, sugar and salt. Beat until the batter has the consistency of cream, adding liquid or flour if needed for thin batter.

Cheese Filling:

2 cups dry cottage cheese
2 tablespoons sour cream
2 extra-large egg yolks

3/4 teaspoon salt
2 tablespoons sugar
1/4 teaspoon vanilla extract

Mix well, taste and adjust the seasonings if needed.

Bread Crumbs and Jelly Filling:

2 cups unseasoned bread crumbs
2 cups milk (more or less depending on dryness of crumbs)
1/2 cup unsalted butter
2 extra-large eggs, well beaten

1 tablespoon honey, or more to taste
1/2 cup finely chopped walnuts
Pinch of grated nutmeg
Pinch of ground cinnamon
Your favorite jelly—ours is raspberry

Mix everything except the jelly. Mold a piece of batter around a teaspoon of jelly.

Lungen Blintzes

Note: *If you can't find lung, a kosher butcher can usually order it for you. It's very tasty. But if the thought of it turns you off, use other meat but without the flour and water paste.*

1 tablespoon flour
2 tablespoons water
1 pound cooked lung meat (2 cups when ground)
1 onion, chopped

1 teaspoon salt or more to taste
1 tablespoon chicken fat
2 extra-large egg yolks

Make a paste of flour and water and stir until smooth. Add the remaining ingredients and mix well.

Making and assembling the blintzes:

To make blintz leaves (*bletlach*) brush a 6-inch frying pan lightly with oil and heat. Pour in just enough batter to cover the bottom—pour off excess if necessary. This takes a little practice—tip the pan to spread the batter all over in a thin layer.

Fry *bletlach* over medium heat for about 2 minutes each, until lightly browned on one side only. Turn out onto paper towels or cloth. Stack them as you go, and with a pastry brush, keep brushing the pan with oil.

Put a spoonful of batter on the cooked side. Fold 1 edge to the center, then fold the opposite edge to meet it. Next, fold the other 2 sides, to make an oblong envelope shape. Do not let filling be exposed.

In a heavy frying pan, heat oil. Carefully place filled blintzes into the pan. Fry until golden brown, turning once to brown both sides crisp.

Matzo Pizza

The summer we worked on Mom's recipes, I had a study group that came to my apartment three times a week. Late one night we sent out for pizza. When Mom came in for lunch the next day, she saw the remnants of it and shuddered. I explained what was in it, but the crust did look awful and was hard as a rock. Her alternative was so successful, we had it once a week on a study night, prepared by her, just ready to pop into the oven. Sometimes we would sneak cheese on the meat ones, or vice versa, feeling very naughty.

There is no recipe, just a procedure. Use one matzo square per person. Spread on tomato sauce, careful to cover all the matzo— exposed dry matzo will burn quickly, like paper.

You can get artistic with slices of mushrooms, shredded cheddar, anchovies, red and green pepper, onion slices and olives, or any combination you like. But don't use cheeses with meat, if it matters to you.

For a meat nosh, use salami, thin slices of frankfurters or even corned beef.

Place under broiler for just 2 to 3 minutes, watching carefully, as it burns quickly. If you use anything that needs slow melting, place it on the lower rack for a few minutes, then transfer to the upper to brown.

Matzo is delicate, so use everything in moderation and thin-sliced. The flavor changes with the type of matzo, whether salt-less, egg and onion, or wheat.

While still hot, it will be soft, so you can cut it into strips. But when it cools, it will get stiff and crisp.

Nahit (Chickpeas)

Like raisins and almonds, you'll often find a bowl of these hanging around a Jewish home to munch on as you would nuts.

They're also known as chickpeas or garbanzos.

1 cup chickpeas	2 tablespoons salt
2 tablespoons vegetable oil	

Soak chickpeas in water overnight. Drain and discard soaking water.

Place the chickpeas in a large pot, cover with water, add oil and salt, and bring to a boil. Reduce heat and simmer for 1 hour or until soft but a little crunchy. Toss with more salt if you like. Serve cold.

Breads

There is no end to the assortment of luscious breads among Jewish foods. The styles and recipes come from all over the globe and have been passed down through the centuries. From plain, satisfying white breads to fancy holiday and dessert ones, bread is treasured. But a few types are traditional fare.

Mom loved to bake bread and she often did it when feeling blue. There is a kind of therapy in the primitive act of kneading and shaping, and the skills involved in timing and temperature.

One of the most cherished universal childhood memories is the aroma of fresh bread throughout the house, mine of course included.

Wheat-Plus Bread

Makes 2 8-inch loaves

The ingredients of this savory bread were snitched off the label of a commercial bread we liked. We added our own touches and now we have the best of both worlds: the taste and security of pure ingredients with no chemicals.

2 envelopes active dry yeast
1/2 cup plus 1 cup lukewarm water, divided
1 cup whole wheat flour
1 cup whole wheat pastry flour
3 cups unbleached flour, or more as needed

1/2 cup bran
2 tablespoons wheat germ
2 teaspoons salt
2 tablespoons honey
1/4 cup prune juice
1/2 cup packed brown sugar
1/4 cup unsalted butter, melted

In a small bowl, dissolve yeast in 1/2 cup lukewarm water. Let stand about 10 minutes or until bubbly.

In a large bowl, mix flours with bran, wheat germ and salt until well blended. Make a well in the center and pour in yeast mixture, remaining water, honey, prune juice, brown sugar and butter. Using your hands or a wooden spoon, mix well, adding additional flour if needed to make a soft dough.

Lightly flour a work surface and grease a large bowl. Grease 2 8-inch loaf pans.

Place dough on the floured surface and knead for 5 minutes, using the heel of the hand and pressing down while rotating the dough; add a bit of flour as needed to keep it from sticking.

Place dough in the greased bowl, and turn so dough is oiled all over. Cover it with a towel and let it stand in a warm spot (85 to 100°) for 1 to 2 hours, or until doubled in volume.

Punch down and knead again for 5 minutes. Divide dough in half. Shape into 2 loaves, transfer to greased loaf pans and let stand until they double in volume again.

Preheat the oven to 375°. Brush loaves with softened butter. Bake for 35 minutes. It will sound hollow when tapped and be nicely brown on top.

Healthy Bagels

Makes 18 to 24

Bagels are a big production to make and it never seemed worth it to me, since store-bought ones are so good and so widely available.

But I was interested in finding out if they could be improved. We made these with whole wheat pastry flour and safflower oil, and sure enough, they *were* better.

We made about 2 dozen. We figured we would have them for the next morning and invite friends to brunch and show off. But by then they were all gone. Mom and I were both avid bread-eaters and had binged on them. I had to rush out to the nearest deli for second-best ones. So if you're making these for company, learn from our experience and control yourself.

Note: *Your oven, heated to 100° for 5 minutes and then turned off, is a good place to let your dough rest.*

1 envelope active dry yeast	2 cups all-purpose flour or
3 tablespoons sugar	more if needed
1 cup lukewarm water or more	2 cups whole wheat pastry
1 extra-large egg	flour
1 extra-large egg,	2 teaspoons salt
separated	1/4 cup safflower oil

In a bowl, dissolve yeast and 1 tablespoon sugar in 1/2 cup lukewarm water. Let stand about 10 minutes.

In a cup bowl, beat whole egg with egg white, oil and remaining water. Reserve yolk for egg wash.

Add flours, salt, 2 tablespoons of sugar and beaten egg and white to yeast mixture and beat well. Put in a greased bowl. Cover with a dishtowel and let stand in a warm, draft-free spot about 1 hour to rise to a spongelike consistency and double in bulk. Test by pressing 2 fingers into it; if you make a depression that stays there, dough is ready for the next step.

Knead on a lightly floured board for 8 to 10 minutes.

Punch down and divide dough into 18 to 24 pieces.

Roll each into a a ball and flatten. Punch a hole in the center of each and shape each cake of dough into a bagel-shape by pulling and rolling. This assures that they won't come apart when boiling.

Bring a large pot of water to a boil, reduce heat to a simmer and drop bagels into the pot—3 to 5 at a time, depending on the size of your pot. Simmer for about 1 minute; then, using a wooden spoon so as not to pierce the dough, turn them over and simmer 1 minute longer. Remove and place on paper or cloth towels to drain and cool, about 5 minutes.

Preheat the oven to 400°. Grease a cookie sheet.

Lay boiled bagels out on the cookie sheet, leaving enough space in between so that they can spread out.

Beat reserved yolk with 1 teaspoon water. Brush tops of bagels with egg wash. If you wish, you can sprinkle with poppy or sesame seeds.

When the bagels begin to rise, bake for about 20 to 30 minutes, until golden brown.

Challah (Egg Bread)

Makes 2 loaves

I could live on this bread. Mom's egg bread was so good, I used to ask her for a regular supply during my crash-study time, as it's emotionally satisfying and very nutritious.

But I began to realize that the bread was getting more and more crumbly and rich until it was more like cake than bread.

I accused her of trying to get me fat. Her idea of giving me extra strength and energy was to keep adding more eggs, butter, milk and sugar.

When we got down to the business of recording the original recipe, she reluctantly cut down on her "remedies."

But you can add a little more butter, or honey, skim milk or even raisins. Use it for rolls or stuffing, or whatever. Bake it by itself on a baking sheet or in a loaf pan.

The pretty braided loaf is the star at sabbath or holiday dinners, so I have included that variation when you feel like fussing.

1 envelope active dry yeast	2 teaspoons salt
2 tablespoons sugar	5 1/2 to 6 cups flour
1/2 cup plus 1 cup lukewarm water, divided	1/4 cup unsalted butter, softened
2 extra-large eggs, beaten	

In a small bowl, dissolve yeast and sugar in 1/2 cup lukewarm water. Let stand about 10 minutes or until bubbly.

In another small bowl, beat eggs with melted butter and remaining water.

In a large bowl, mix salt and flour. Make a well in the center and pour in egg and yeast mixtures. Using your hands or a wooden spoon, gradually incorporate liquids into flour, adding more flour if needed to make a soft dough.

Lightly flour a work surface and grease a large bowl.

Place dough on the floured surface and knead for 5 minutes, using the heel of the hand and pressing down while rotating the dough; add flour as needed to keep it from sticking.

Put dough in a greased bowl, rotate dough so it is oiled all over, cover it with a towel and let it stand in a warm spot (85 to 100°) for 1 to 2 hours, until doubled in volume.

Punch down and knead again for another 5 minutes. Shape into 2 loaves, place in 2 9-inch greased loaf pans and let stand until they double in volume again. Brush with softened butter. Preheat the oven to 375° and bake for 40 to 50 minutes. It will sound hollow when tapped and be nicely brown on top.

Note: *For braided loaves, divide dough in two sections and keep half covered. Divide the second half into 3 even pieces. Roll each on a lightly floured work surface to make a 16-inch rope. Arrange the 3 ropes lengthwise on a large cookie sheet and braid. Pinch and turn the ends under the loaf to keep them from opening. Repeat with remaining dough. Cover both with a towel and let rise in a warm spot for about 30 minutes, until they double in volume again.*

Brush with egg yolk diluted with water and sprinkle lightly with poppy or sesame seeds. Transfer to greased baking sheet and bake as directed above.

Rutele's
Oatmeal Bread

Makes 2 loaves

This is named after me because for a while, I got on a health food kick and read that oatmeal is a super food. I urged Mom to eat it, convincing her that Grandma Moses was painting pictures at age 90 because she ate a bowl of oatmeal every morning.

So the next step was to throw it into bread, our mainstay, in a very successful experiment.

1 envelope active dry yeast
2 cups lukewarm water or
   more
5 1/4 to 5 1/2 cups flour
2 teaspoons salt
1 cup rolled oats

1/4 teaspoon ground
   cinnamon
1/4 cup packed brown sugar
2 tablespoons unsalted butter
1/2 cup raisins

In a small bowl, dissolve yeast in 1/2 cup of the lukewarm water. Let stand about 10 minutes or until bubbly.

In a large bowl, mix flour with salt, oats and cinnamon until well blended. Make a well in the center and pour in yeast mixture remaining water, brown sugar and butter. Add raisins. Using your hands or a wooden spoon, mix well, adding more flour if needed to make a soft dough.

Lightly flour a work surface and grease a large bowl. Grease 2 8-inch loaf pans.

Place dough on the floured surface and knead for 5 minutes, using the heel of the hand and pressing down while rotating the dough; add a bit of flour as needed to keep it from sticking. Place dough in the greased bowl, and turn so dough is oiled all over, cover it with a towel and let it stand in a warm spot (85 to 100°) for 1 to 2 hours, or until doubled in volume.

Punch down and knead again for 5 minutes. Divide dough in half. Shape into 2 loaves, transfer to greased loaf pans and let stand until they double in volume again.

Preheat the oven to 375°. Bake for 35 minutes. It will sound hollow when tapped and be nicely brown on top.

Raisin-Nut Swirl Bread

Makes 1 loaf

You can use any bread recipe you like, or make rolls, and use this recipe to dress them up. We used half the challah recipe for 1 loaf. Proceed as for regular bread, with this filling and method.

Dough for 1/2 challah recipe, page 129
3 tablespoons softened unsalted butter
1 extra-large egg, beaten

1/4 cup packed brown sugar
1/2 teaspoon ground cinnamon
1/2 cup finely chopped raisins
1/4 cup finely chopped pecans

Prepare challah dough.
Grease a 9-inch loaf pan.
Mix all the ingredients well.
Roll dough into a 9-by-16-inch rectangle and spread filling on it. Roll up, pinch edges together and place in loaf pan with pinched side down. Cover with a towel and let rise for 30 minutes. Bake as for challah.

Date-Nut Bread

Makes 1 loaf

Everybody should have a good recipe for a fruit bread—for noshing or celebration meals or just to treat a special guest. Here is a top class one. But it's no secret that it's more like a cake than a bread.

3/4 cup dates
1/4 cup prunes
1 teaspoon vanilla extract
1/2 teaspoon orange extract
1/2 teaspoon lemon extract
1 cup boiling water
2 extra-large eggs, beaten
2 tablespoons unsalted butter

1 1/4 cup hard packed brown
  sugar
2 cups flour
1 teaspoon baking soda
1/2 teaspoon baking powder
1 teaspoon salt
1/2 cup coarsely chopped
  walnuts

Preheat the oven to 325°. Grease an 8-inch loaf pan and line it with waxed paper.

Snip dates and prunes into little pieces. Combine with vanilla, orange, and lemon extract, boiling water and eggs and let stand 15 minutes.

Beat butter and sugar. Add flour, baking soda, baking powder and salt, then add the prune mixture and mix, until blended into a thick batter. Stir in nuts.

Spoon batter into pan and bake 1 hour and 10 minutes, until a cake tester inserted into the loaf comes out clean.

Desserts

Jewish cookery abounds with tantalizing desserts, mostly baked goods and lots of fruits. At least, these were the standards at our house and circle of landsleit (countrymen). I could never sell Mom on desserts made with gelatin, or anything else that jiggled. Don't ask me why, she couldn't explain it herself. She just didn't trust food that moved.

Anyway, the fragrance of the baked desserts through the house and down the block made up for the lack of variety. I'm sure you will agree when you have tried some of the following treats.

Ambrosia Cheesecake

With cheesecake, you might as well forget diets, except when made with butter substitutes, skim milk, low-fat cheeses or other blah-tasting stuff.

Or you can go another way and use the recipe as it is, but only eat a sliver, surrounded by lots of fresh, pretty fruit so you would not feel too guilty.

Crust:

1 1/2 cups graham cracker crumbs
1/2 cup ground almonds
1/2 cup unsalted butter, melted
2 tablespoons packed brown sugar

1 extra-large egg, slightly beaten
1/2 teaspoon ground cinnamon
1/4 teaspoon cardamom

Cheesecake Batter:

12 ounces cream cheese
2 tablespoons flour
1 teaspoon vanilla extract
2 tablespoons lemon juice
1 teaspoon grated lemon rind
4 extra-large eggs, well beaten

1 cup sugar
2 tablespoons shredded coconut
1 cup sour cream
2 tablespoons rum

To make the crust, grease a 9-inch springform pan. Mix ingredients well.

Press crust into prepared pan, half-way up.

Preheat the oven to 350°.

Mix cheesecake batter ingredients well and pour into crust. Bake for 45 minutes. Turn off heat and leave the cake in the oven with the door open for 45 minutes.

Trim with strawberries and pineapple wedges. Glaze with melted apricot jelly.

Easy Strudel

The origin of strudel is unknown, but it is most popular with Hungarians, Romanians and Viennese.

Mom had patience for other things, but not for making the paper thin stretched dough. She used the easier, rolled dough.

Note: *The fats, juice or water and egg should be cold; the other ingredients should be at room temperature.*

2 cups flour, or more or less as
    needed
1 teaspoon baking powder
1/2 teaspoon salt
2 tablespoons sugar
1/4 cup butter
1 extra-large egg
1/2 teaspoon vanilla extract
1/2 teaspoon lemon extract
1/2 cup water, or more or less
    as needed
Unsalted butter, melted
Apple-Poppy Seed Filling
3 to 4 tablespoons cream

Preheat the oven to 350°. Lightly grease an 8-by-8-inch baking pan.

In a large bowl, combine the flour, baking powder, salt and sugar. Cut in butter and, using your hands, combine until the mixture has the consistency of coarse meal.

In a separate bowl, beat egg with vanilla and lemon extract and add it to the flour mixture. Add water a little at a time until you have a soft, but not sticky, ball of dough. Divide in half.

Roll each half into a rectangle 8 inches wide. Spread with the filling and roll up. Pinch the overlapped dough so it won't spread during baking and place in pan. Brush with melted butter.

Bake for about 40 minutes. Cool for at least 1 hour and cut into 1-inch portions.

Apple-Poppy Seed Filling:

1/2 cup poppy seeds
1/2 cup tart apple, peeled and
    cored
1/2 cup raisins
1/2 cup walnuts
1/4 cup sugar
1/4 cup honey
1/4 teaspoon ground
    cinnamon
1 teaspoon grated lemon rind

Using a food processor or a mortar and pestle, grind seeds and set aside. Next, process or finely mince apple, raisins and walnuts.

Transfer seeds, fruit and nuts to a mixing bowl. Add sugar, honey, cinnamon and lemon rind and combine until well mixed.

Banana-Nut Cake

Very similar to Date-Nut Bread, except of course, another taste and softer. Everybody is crazy about this, especially with whipped cream on top, and a banana slice on top of that (dipped in lemon juice to prevent discoloring) and maybe even a cherry on top for pretty.

1/2 cup unsalted butter, softened	1 3/4 cups flour
3/4 cup hard packed brown sugar	1 teaspoon baking powder
	1 teaspoon baking soda
2 extra-large eggs	1/2 teaspoon salt
1 teaspoon vanilla extract	1 cup (about 2 large ripe) mashed bananas
1/2 teaspoon lemon extract	1/2 cup coarsely chopped nuts
1/2 teaspoon grated lemon rind	

Preheat the oven to 350°. Grease an 8-inch loaf pan.

Cream butter and sugar until light and fluffy. Beat in eggs, vanilla and lemon extract. Blend in dry ingredients and mix but do not beat.

Add bananas and nuts, mixing until blended.

Bake 35 to 45 minutes, until a cake tester inserted in the center comes out clean. Cool before slicing. If you can, it's best to refrigerate the cake overnight.

Honey Cake

Known as *lekach*, this cake is a classic, so the ingredients do not vary much from baker to baker, but individual cooks manage to make theirs unique. Some like it more dry; others prefer moist. The flavors vary a bit. Whatever; it should be a firm loaf.

4 extra-large eggs
1/2 cup white sugar
1/4 cup packed brown sugar
1 1/2 cups honey
1 cup strong brewed coffee
3 tablespoons rum
1/2 teaspoon vanilla extract
1/4 cup vegetable oil
3 1/4 cups flour
2 teaspoons baking powder
1 teaspoon baking soda

1/2 teaspoon salt
1/2 teaspoon ground cinnamon
1/2 teaspoon ground ginger
1/4 teaspoon grated nutmeg
1/4 teaspoon cardamom
1/4 teaspoon allspice
1 cup chopped nuts
1/2 cup currants
1 tablespoon grated orange rind

Preheat oven to 325°. Lightly grease 2 8-inch loaf pans and line them with waxed paper.

Beat eggs. Add sugars and mix well. Add honey, coffee and rum. Beat well. Add oil. Blend in flour, baking soda, salt, cinnamon, ginger, nutmeg, cardamom, allspice and combine. Add nuts, currants and orange rind, and mix well.

Pour batter into prepared pans. Bake for 1 hour or until a cake tester inserted in the center of the cake comes out clean.

Raisin Cake

Truthfully, I was never crazy about this cake, but it was Mom's favorite and she baked it constantly. Everyone else loved it, so it wouldn't be fair to leave it out of her collection. I have no idea where it came from and she couldn't remember.

1 cup raisins
3/4 cup water
1 teaspoon baking soda
1/2 cup unsalted butter,
    melted
3/4 cup sugar
2 extra-large eggs, well beaten
2 tablespoons brandy

2 cups flour
1/2 teaspoon baking powder
1/2 teaspoon salt
1/2 cup nuts
Orange marmalade, melted,
    for glaze
Sliced almonds

Soak raisins in water and baking soda for several hours.

Preheat the oven to 325°. Use a little of the melted butter to grease 8-inch loaf pan.

Pour remaining melted butter into a large bowl. Add sugar and beat well. Beat in 1 egg at a time. Add brandy.

In another bowl, combine the flour, baking powder and salt and add the dry mixture to the batter. Add the nuts. Transfer batter to the prepared pan.

Glaze the top with melted orange marmalade and sprinkle with sliced almonds.

Bake for 45 minutes to 1 hour, until a cake tester inserted into the center comes out clean.

Sponge Cake

It took about a dozen tries until I got it right, but sponge cake is one of the most versatile and popular of all cakes, and well worth the trouble. The secret is in having all the ingredients at room temperature—and—listen carefully—beat the yolks to a sponge until they are cream-colored. That's the reason for the name. (The finished cake also has the texture of sponge.) You can make this cake in any number of shapes and sizes, and you can serve it many delicious ways. This recipe is my favorite.

At one party, we discovered a huge bite out of one side of a perfect cake we had just finished and displayed on the sideboard. We immediately accused the children of stealing nibbles, but they claimed innocence. Later they whispered to us to come and look: Pesita, our cat, had discovered the joys of nibbling sponge cake. So we can truly say that everyone loves this recipe.

Note: You can bake this cake in a 10-inch tube pan, or two 9-inch loaf pans, or two 9-inch round cake pans, or three 8-inch round cake pans. Trim the finished cake with glazed fruit, and/or fill layers with whipped cream. Or toast it in squares and serve it with a sauce.

9 extra-large eggs, separated	1/4 teaspoon cream of tartar
1 1/4 cups sugar	1/2 teaspoon salt
1 1/2 cups flour	1 teaspoon grated orange rind
1 1/2 teaspoons baking	Sugar
powder	Trimming
1/2 cup orange juice	

Preheat the oven to 325°.

Beat yolks for about 3 minutes until light colored and spongy. Add 1 cup of the sugar and beat 2 minutes longer.

In a separate bowl, combine flour and baking powder and add, little by little, to yolks, alternating with small amounts of orange juice.

Beat egg whites with cream of tartar for about 5 minutes until it forms stiff peaks. Add salt, the remaining 1/4 cup sugar and orange rind. Beat until well combined.

Fold whites into yolk mixture and pour into an *ungreased* 10-inch tube pan but grease or line bottom. Sprinkle lightly with sugar for delicate crust.

Bake for at least 1 hour, or until a caketester inserted in the center comes out clean. Invert the pan to cool for at least 1 hour. Ease the cake out of the pan with a spatula or sharp knife.

Trimming:

1 cup sifted confectioner's sugar	pineapple chunks, cherries
1 to 2 teaspoons milk, or more	or whatever you wish
as needed	Apricot jelly, melted and
Canned or fresh fruit such as	diluted, optional, for glaze
apricot halves, plum halves,	

To trim the sponge cake, mix confectioner's sugar with a little milk (start with 1 to 2 teaspoons—it gets gooey very quickly). Blend until the icing mixture is smooth and of slow-dripping consistency. Spread a layer of icing on top of cake and let it drip down the sides like icicles, leaving about 2 inches between them.

Then, arrange pieces of canned or fresh fruit in a pretty design on top of cake; dry off the bottoms so they will stick well.

If you like a glaze, you can paint the fruit with one made of melted and diluted apricot jelly.

Cherry Cake

An age-old cake like this usually appears in ethnic cookbooks as apple cake. It's made with either a cookie or sweet biscuit or shortcake dough and pieces of fresh fruit, in either one or two layers. It's best known as Old World apple cake, but we found that cherries are marvelous with a cookie dough and pie-type filling.

Our version is an informal dump-it-in method. It's a cross between a cake and a pie, in fact. But don't make it unless you can find gorgeous, sweet cherries. If not, use another great-tasting fruit, or, second best, use your favorite canned fruit.

2 1/4 cups flour	2 extra-large eggs, beaten
1/3 cup sugar, or more or less	1/2 teaspoon salt
as needed	1/2 teaspoon vanilla extract
1 1/2 teaspoons baking	1/4 teaspoon almond extract
powder	Cherry Filling Streusel
1/2 cup unsalted butter	Mixture, optional

Preheat the oven to 350°. Grease a 9-by-9-inch baking pan.

Mix flour, sugar and baking powder. Cut in butter. Work in eggs, vanilla and almond extract and mix until a soft ball of dough forms. Press half of it into prepared pan.

Put the cherry mixture on top of the dough in the pan. Roll or pat the remaining dough and place on top.

If you wish, spread Streusel Mixture evenly over the cake.

Bake for about 50 minutes until dough is just baked through. Serve hot or cold.

Cherry Filling:

4 cups cherries, about 1 1/2	1 tablespoon cornstarch
pounds	1 teaspoon lemon juice
1/2 cup sugar, more or less	1/4 cup water
depending on the sweetness	
of the fruit	

To prepare the cherry filling, in a medium saucepan, cook the cherries, sugar, flour or cornstarch, lemon juice, water and butter over medium heat for about 3 minutes, until thickened to desired consistency. Adjust texture by adding liquid or cornstarch. Adjust flavor to taste.

If you wish, top it with the following streusel mixture:

Streusel mixture:

1/4 cup hard packed brown sugar
2 tablespoons flour
1/2 cup walnuts, chopped fine
1/4 teaspoon ground cinnamon

1/8 teaspoon grated nutmeg
3 to 4 tablespoons unsalted butter, melted

Combine all the ingredients.

Marble Nut Coffee Cake

A true coffee cake is made with a yeast dough, but this quick one is just as scrumptious, if not more. I like it so much that I often treat it like a tube cake and trim it with frosting and chocolate curls for a fancy affair.

This recipe makes a flat cake topped with streusel and cut in squares.

White Batter:

1/2 cup unsalted butter, softened
1 cup sugar
2 extra-large eggs, lightly beaten
1 cup sour cream

1 1/2 teaspoons baking powder
1 teaspoon vanilla extract
1 1/2 cups flour
1 teaspoon baking soda
1/4 teaspoon salt

Preheat the oven to 350°. Lightly grease a 9-by-9-inch baking pan.

Cream butter and sugar well until light and fluffy. Blend in eggs, one at a time. Mix sour cream with baking soda and add to the egg mixture. Mix well. Add the rest of the ingredients and beat for 2 minutes or 200 strokes.

Remove 1 cup of the batter and add the following ingredients to it:

Chocolate Batter:

1/4 cup cocoa
3/4 teaspoon lemon extract
1 tablespoon rum
1/2 cup hard packed brown
  sugar
1/2 teaspoon ground
  cinnamon

2 tablespoons unsalted butter,
  melted
3 tablespoons finely chopped
  walnuts
3 tablespoons finely chopped
  raisins

Spoon half of the white batter into prepared pan. Pour the chocolate mixture in the center and add the rest of the white mixture on top.

Drag the tip of a sharp knife through the batter to make a marble design.

Top with the streusel.

Streusel:

1/3 cup hard packed brown
  sugar
1/3 cup flour
1/2 teaspoon ground
  cinnamon

1/4 teaspoon grated nutmeg
3/4 cup nuts, finely chopped
2 tablespoons unsalted butter,
  melted

Combine and mix well.

Bake for 45 minutes, until the tip of a sharp knife inserted in the center comes out clean. Leave in the oven with the door open for an hour.

Apple Pie Supreme

Mom made the best apple pie ever. But it was never exactly the same, except for the cookie crust, walnuts and spices. Sometimes it was a little runny, sometimes very thick. You'll have to experiment because the texture varies with the kind of apples you use. For uniform results, though, you can use a favorite brand of frozen apples and adjust the sweetener and flavors.

Note: For the crust, the fats, juice or water, and egg should be cold; the other ingredients should be at room temperature. For the filling, use just enough water or juice to moisten the apples if they are dry.

Crust:

2 1/2 cups flour
1/2 teaspoon baking powder
1/4 teaspoon salt
2 tablespoons sugar
1/4 cup unsalted butter
1/4 cup vegetable shortening

1 extra-large egg
1 teaspoon vanilla extract
1 teaspoon grated lemon rind
About 6 tablespoons, more or
   less ice water

Filling:

4 to 5 cooking apples, peeled,
   cored and thinly sliced
2 tablespoons sugar
3 to 4 tablespoons water or
   apple juice or orange juice

1/4 teaspoon salt
2 tablespoons flour
1/4 cup chopped walnuts

Topping:

1/4 teaspoon ground
   cinnamon
1/2 teaspoon sugar

1/4 cup bread crumbs
2 tablespoons butter
2 tablespoons raspberry jam

Preheat the oven to 450°. Lightly butter the bottom of a glass pie plate.

In a large bowl, combine flour, baking powder, salt and sugar. Cut in butter and shortening with a pastry blender and combine until the mixture has the consistency of coarse meal.

In a separate bowl, beat egg with vanilla and lemon rind and add it to the mixture. Working quickly, add water or juice a little at a time until you have a soft, but not sticky ball of dough. Divide dough in half.

On a lightly floured surface, roll half the dough until it is 1/8 inch thick.

Carefully lift the dough and line the prepared pie plate with it. Trim the edges leaving a 1-inch overlap.

Meanwhile, prepare the filling by mixing all of the ingredients well. Dust the bottom of pan with a little sugar and flour, then fill crust with apple mixture.

Combine cinnamon, sugar and bread crumbs and sprinkle over the apple mixture. Dot topping with 2 tablespoons butter and 2 tablespoons raspberry jam.

Roll out the rest of the dough until it is 1/8 inch thick. From here, you can either cut it into strips to make a lattice pattern on top of the pie, or roll the dough flat and cover pie with the whole piece, making slits on top. Turn overlap to inside and pinch top and bottom crusts together making a decorative edge.

Bake for 15 minutes. Reduce temperature to 350° and bake for 35 to 45 minutes more. Watch carefully and cover with foil if pie is browning too quickly.

Peaches and Cream Pie

Unless you can find very good tasting peaches, it's safer to use canned ones for this pie. But as in all the other recipes, you have to adjust the sugar depending on the taste of the fruit, also the juiciness.

What makes this different is the cream. A terrific touch is to use lots of pecan halves, either in the filling or as trimming on top.

Note: *This crust is half of the Apple Pie Supreme crust.*

Crust:

1 1/4 cups flour
1/4 teaspoon baking powder
1/8 teaspoon salt
1 tablespoon sugar
2 tablespoons unsalted butter
2 tablespoons vegetable
   shortening

1 extra-large egg yolk
1/2 teaspoon vanilla extract
1/2 teaspoon grated lemon
   rind
About 3 tablespoons ice water,
   more or less

Filling:

3 cups sliced peaches or
   halves, drained and dried
1/4 cup sugar

2 tablespoons flour
1/4 teaspoon salt
1/2 cup cream

Preheat the oven to 425°. Lightly butter the bottom of a glass pie plate.

In a large bowl, combine flour, baking powder, salt and sugar. Cut in butter and shortening with a pastry blender and combine until the mixture has the consistency of coarse meal.

In a separate bowl, beat egg with vanilla and lemon rind and add it to the mixture. Working quickly, add water or juice a little at a time until you have a soft, but not sticky, ball of dough.

On a lightly floured surface, roll dough until it is 1/8 inch thick.

Carefully lift the dough and line the prepared pie plate with it. Trim the edges.

Arrange the fruit in a design in the pan.

Beat remaining ingredients and pour over fruit.

Bake for 10 minutes, then reduce the temperature to 350° and bake for 35 minutes or more, until crust is golden brown. If it browns too fast, cover with foil. Pies are tricky that way.

Taiglach

Makes 3 dozen or more

In the old country, peasant life was simple but evidently healthy, since my great-grandmother lived 107 years. My grandmother left my mother's house to remarry at age 81!

Food was simple and fresh, and many delicacies given in this book were made only during holidays. *Taiglach* are among these.

It's a nuisance to make and I'm not even sure it's worth it, but I have to tell you, once you start eating them, it's hard to quit.

Dough:

1 3/4 to 2 cups flour	3 tablespoons vegetable oil
1/4 teaspoon salt	1 tablespoon brandy
1 teaspoon baking powder	2 tablespoons lemon juice
3 extra-large eggs	

Syrup:

1 cup honey
1/2 cup sugar
2 tablespoons lemon juice
1 teaspoon ground ginger
1 cup coarsely chopped
  walnuts

Cherries, pitted and diced,
  optional
Crystallized ginger, chopped,
  optional
Shredded coconut, optional

Preheat the oven to 375°.

Combine flour, salt and baking powder.

Beat eggs. Add oil, brandy and 2 tablespoons lemon juice. Combine the flour mixture and the egg mixture and work into a dough. Knead until smooth.

Divide the dough in half and roll each half into tubes 1/2 inch thick. Cut these into 1/2-inch pieces.

Bake for 10 minutes until light brown, shaking every few minutes to brown evenly. Remove from the oven and cool.

In a large saucepan, boil honey, sugar, 2 tablespoons lemon juice and ginger and simmer 10 to 15 minutes, watching carefully. Add pastry pieces, 6 to 8 at a time. Add nuts.

Reduce heat and simmer for about 5 minutes, until golden brown. The pastry—taiglach—will rise to surface when done.

With a slotted spoon, take out a few taiglach at a time and place on a wet board. With wet hands, shape into small balls, with 3 to 4 taiglach each and some nuts.

If you wish, you can also add cut up cherries, crystallized ginger in tiny pieces, molding them into the balls with wet hands, and/or dust at the finish with coconut.

Jewel Cookies

Makes 2 dozen

This is not just a pretty cookie; it's also melt-in-your-mouth delicious.

Its versatility is endless. You can vary the size or shape, or make a refrigerator roll. With a little more flour it can be rolled and cut into shapes with a cookie cutter.

This recipe makes 2 dozen very tender tidbits.
Note: *Be sure to use the egg yolk only.*

1/2 cup very finely minced
    pecans
1 cup plus 2 tablespoons flour
1/2 teaspoon salt
1/2 cup unsalted butter

1/3 cup sugar
1 extra-large egg yolk
1 teaspoon vanilla extract
Jelly in assorted colors (red,
    green, yellow, orange)

Preheat the oven to 350°. Grease a cookie sheet.

Dust pecans lightly with a little wflour. Mix flour with salt. Cream butter and sugar, add yolk and vanilla, and mix well.

Divide batter into 24 pieces, roll into balls, then press each down on a cookie sheet until 1/4 inch thick.

With your thumb or the handle of a large wooden spoon, make a dent in the center of each cookie, almost to the bottom but not all the way through or the jelly will leak out. Spoon about 1/8 teaspoon jelly into each depression, using different-colored jellies.

Bake for 15 minutes.

Poppy Seed Squares

Makes 25 squares

This is another way to use these delectable seeds. For many baked goods, poppy seeds must be pounded to bring out the flavor or bought pre-ground in gourmet or specialty shops. In these cookies they are used as is.

1/2 cup unsalted butter
1/4 cup sugar
1/4 cup hard packed brown
    sugar
1 extra-large egg
1 teaspoon vanilla extract
1/4 teaspoon almond extract

1 3/4 flour, or a little more if
    needed
1 teaspoon baking powder
1/2 teaspoon salt
3 tablespoons poppy seeds
1/2 teaspoon cardamom

Preheat the oven to 350°.

Cream butter and sugars. Add egg, vanilla and almond extract and mix well. Add remaining ingredients. Add more flour if needed, until dough doesn't stick to wooden board or work surface.

Roll or pat into a 3/8-inch thick 10-inch square. Cut into 2-inch squares. Bake for 10 to 12 minutes, until the edges of the squares are brown.

Passover
Double Nut Macaroons

Makes 36 small macaroons

You can make a big impression with macaroons and with very little effort. All you need is a couple of egg whites and something to add like nuts, shredded coconut or candied fruit. We made them often since we had recipes that called for yolks only, such as Jewel Cookies or Egg Noodles.

In this recipe, we couldn't decide whether to use almonds or walnuts, so my inventive mother suggested both—with unusually great results.

Note: *Starting with egg whites at room temperature will produce the greatest volume.*

2 extra-large egg whites at room temperature	1/2 cup *fine* sugar
1/8 teaspoon salt	2 tablespoons matzo *cake* meal
1/8 teaspoon cream of tartar	1/2 cup ground almonds
	1/2 cup finely minced walnuts

Preheat the oven to 350°. Cover 2 baking sheets with brown paper and grease the paper well.

Beat whites with salt and cream of tartar until foamy. Then, while still beating, gradually add sugar. Continue beating until the mixture forms stiff peaks.

Carefully fold in the matzo meal and nuts.

Drop by teaspoons into little mounds on prepared baking sheets.

Bake for about 15 minutes.

Remove the pan from the oven and immediately insert a piece of wet cloth or paper towel under the brown paper and let stand a few minutes until cookies come off easily.

Cool and store in an airtight container. Macaroons are best if "ripened" a few days before eating—if you can control yourself.

Pink Applesauce

One Valentine's Day I was a loner and snubbed a depression by throwing a pot luck party for the friends I loved. Mom qualified and offered her utility applesauce. I told her that I asked everyone to bring food that had a pink or red touch, or was heart-shaped.

Getting into the spirit, she obliged with pink applesauce in a deep glass bowl surrounded by heart-shaped cookies with pink and red sprinkles.

About 5 apples, (about 5 cups), each one peeled, cored and cut in 8 pieces
2 cups cranberries

2 cups water
2 teaspoons lemon juice
Honey to taste

Place apples and cranberries into a large pot, cover with water and simmer until tender. If you like chunky applesauce, mash with potato masher. For smoother sauce, press through a sieve.

Add lemon juice and honey while still hot and mix well.

Honey Wine Fruit Compote

Serves 6

Ridiculously simple to make for something this good and this wholesome. It's a marvelous accompaniment to a plain cake such as sponge cake.

6 cups mixed fresh fruit
1/4 cup honey
1/4 cup boiling water

1/4 to 1/2 cup wine, depending on taste and strength

Place the fruit in a pretty glass bowl. Melt honey in boiled water and pour over fruit. Mix gently and let stand until cool. Add wine.

Stuffed Dates

Try to find big plump dates such as Empress or Medjul in specialty stores. If these are not available, use regular market-variety Deglet Noors. Remove the pits, stick two together and then stuff. They shouldn't look skimpy. Here are two ideas:

1. Spread inside with peanut butter. Place a big Brazil nut inside. Roll in sugar.
2. Finely chop crystallized ginger fine and mix with cream cheese and finely chopped walnuts or pecans. Roll in sugar or finely shredded coconut.

Stuffed Prunes

Your artistic taste can be expressed with lots of different things added to dates or prunes. But certain things go better with one than the other. This is a great one for prunes.

1/4 cup finely chopped pecans
4 large marshmallows, snipped into little pieces
6 maraschino cherries, chopped
2 tablespoons mayonnaise
1/2 pound jumbo prunes, steamed until plump but not too soft

Mix pecans, marshmallows, cherries and mayonnaise. Stuff prunes and roll each in sugar.

Passover Cupcakes

Makes 24 cupcakes

This is a sponge cake, but it's different in that it doesn't use flour, which is not permitted at Passover. It's entered in this book to show you that the *Pesach* way of baking is just as tasty, and what to substitute. Once you've mastered the skill of sponge cake, you'll make it all your life.

1/2 cup matzo cake meal
1/2 cup potato starch
6 extra-large eggs, separated,
  and at room temperature
1/4 teaspoon salt
1 1/4 cups sugar
1/3 cup hot water

2 tablespoons orange juice
3 tablespoons lemon juice
2 teaspoons grated orange rind
2 teaspoons lemon rind
1/2 teaspoon vanilla extract
1/4 cup finely chopped or
  ground nuts

Preheat the oven to 325°. Grease the bottoms of 2 12-cup muffin tins.

Sift matzo meal and potato starch three times.

Beat whites with salt and 1/4 cup of the sugar until it forms stiff peaks.

Beat yolks, water and juices for about 5 minutes, until the mixture has a spongy consistency. Add dry ingredients and mix well. Add orange and lemon rind and nuts and mix. Fold in the whites gently.

Pour batter into prepared muffin tins, filling each cup about 3/4 to 7/8 full.

Bake 20 to 25 minutes.

Note: *Sponge cake is drier than butter cakes, so it is usually served with a fruit sauce, fruit compote, or trimmed with fruit and/or topped with whipped cream. A nice way to trim these cupcakes is with a half peach on top and glazed with melted apricot jelly.*

Menus

Keep in mind that in all recipes given, parts are interchangeable. For instance, tomato soup with rice can also be served with farfel, matzo balls, store-bought mandlen, and so forth. Stuffings are also interchangeable, mostly.

Shabbis and Big Dinners

From sundown Friday to sundown Saturday, tradition rules a full day of rest. In orthodox homes, the house has been scrubbed to sparkle and troubles are put aside. Peace and good will rule the day.

My folks and their friends did not follow all the rules of shabbis, but I always think of Friday night as the time when parents tried to get the kids together for dinner, luring them with food favorites and interesting friends.

Making it an event is a wonderful psychological custom. Looking forward to a family get-together is a blessing for parents, especially widowed, old and lonely ones. When my mother knew that even one child would be over on a Friday (or any other night), it calmed her anxiety and kept her busy for days preparing special foods without thinking of saving time with instant foods and quickie meals. And it was one pleasurable way to express her creativity.

Special events for my mother included family dinners, and the table groaned with an army of dishes. Not an inch of the table was left uncovered. So shabbis and big dinners are grouped together and are really interchangeable.

#1	*#2*
Herring balls	Chopped eggs and onions in
Radishes	celery stalks
Roast capon-peach stuffing	Nahit
Potato kugelach	Lamb roast—served hot
Beefsteak tomato salad	Rice pudding
Asparagus	Artichokes
Stewed fruit	Banana nut cake
Raisin cake	Fresh fruit bowl
Challah	Oatmeal bread
Tea and lemon	Tea and lemon

#3

Chopped liver
Celery and carrot sticks
Brisket Stew with potatoes,
Carrots and onions
Spinach salad
Peach pie—made with
    orange juice
Toasted egg bread
Cream soda or tea

#4

Cream cheese creations
Tomato rice soup
Fish Cakes and cream sauce
Sweet corn
Stuffed mushrooms
Strudel
Strawberry ice cream
Healthy bagels
Coffee or tea

#5

Pickles
Black olives
Cold borscht
Sauteed Salmon
Mint peas (fresh peas
    cooked with mint, salt
    and sugar)
baked potato
Salad: half avocado
    on lettuce, oil
    and vinegar dressing
Apple pie—vanilla ice cream
Rolls made with challah recipe
tea or coffee

#6

Gefilte fish
Half grapefruit
Capoosta
Sliced tomato and cucumber salad
Sponge cake, apricot and plum
    topping, glazed
Lemon-lime soda or tea

Holiday Dinners

There is no attempt in this book to follow orthodox rules or even to explain them. There are many excellent books on the subject. But just a sketchy idea will serve the purpose of acquainting the beginner with the basic ideas of the holidays. There is no exact time for the celebrations, since the complex Jewish calendar doesn't correspond with the common one.

Purim (Usually in March, sometimes late February). Purim is an historical festivity, celebrating the survival of Jews and Judaism under the ancient Persian King Ahasuerus and his queen, Esther, a Jew. His villainous minister Hamen proclaimed that everyone must bow to him. Mordecai, Esther's cousin, refused. As a faithful

Jew, he could only bow to God. The enraged Hamen sentenced the entire Hebrew population to death. Esther, after prayer and fasting, exposed Hamen to the king and pleaded for her people. The king had Hamen put to death on the very day the Jews were to be extinguished. The date had been chosen by the casting of lots, the Persian word *purim*. Thus, Purim is known as the Festival of Lots and is a happy holiday with games and gifts and feasting.

Purim Dinner
Stuffed eggs with lox
Split pea soup with mandlen
Stuffed whole fish
Rice pudding
Wheat plus bread
Honey glazed varrots
Raisins and almonds
Sour cream and minced vegetables
Sponge cake
Honey wine fruit compote
Tea or coffee

Passover (Pesach) (Usually in April). Another historical holiday, this is the Festival of Freedom, celebrating the Hebrews' flight from Egypt and out of bondage, led by Moses. The name is from the story of the angel, who when visiting various plagues and punishments on the Egyptians, passed over the Jewish homes and spared the first born of the Israelites.

This is the only holiday during which special foods are required. It is the time of *matzo,* (unleavened bread), because during the flight there was no time for bread to rise. So leavening is also forbidden, along with grains, legumes or garlic. Flour in baking is replaced by matzo meal, matzo cake meal and potato starch and you will see recipes with many eggs as leavening.

The ceremony of the first seder—the ritual Passover meal—is long and complex, and without a presiding person who is trained for the occasion, it may be anything from slightly disorganized to a mess, the way I experienced it many times. It can also go on for hours, as ritual is observed by the reading of the *Haggadah*, the story of the Exodus, drinking of wine, and some adults and even children can get pretty hungry and a little smashed. So it's a good idea to have a late lunch or a nosh in between. But it's always a rousing good time, although not diet time. I've included two meals because it is an eight-day holiday. The use of matzo is not a deprivation, because it's very tasty. I have it around all year as my favorite cracker-food.

#1	#2
Gefilte fish	Chopped herring
Chopped eggs with olives	Fresh fruit cup
Chicken Soup with matzo balls	Tomato soup, matzo farfel
Tsimmis, meat and vegetables	Stuffed breast of veal
Potato kugel	Mix of broccoli and mushrooms
Lettuce wedges, anchovies	Carrot raisin salad
Russian dressing	Stuffed dates
Passover sponge cake,	Passover double nut macaroons
Glazed fruit topping	Pink applesauce
Matzos	Matzos
Tea and assorted sodas	Tea and celery tonic

Rosh Hashonah (usually late September or early October). This is the Day of Judgment and begins the Jewish New Year, also the High Holy Days, ending with Yom Kippur, the Day of Atonement, and a day of fasting. It is a profound 10-day holiday focusing on contemplation, solemn prayer, self-examination, and penitence, but also inner peace and joy. Orthodox people make peace with others if harm was involved. Forgiveness and a fresh start is the order of the day.

Food is traditional and symbolic. A bowl of honey is served, and apples and challah are dipped in it, signifying a sweet New Year.

Rosh Hashonah Dinner

Chopped Liver
Chicken soup with noodles

Duck with peach stuffing
Honey glazed ginger carrots
String beans

Beet Mandarin salad

Honey cake
Stewed fruit in honey wine sauce

Egg bread

Tea and lemon

Sukkos (usually late September or early October). Sukkos is the Jewish Thanksgiving, the celebration of the harvest, known as the Festival of the Booths or Tabernacles. It's a seven- to nine-day holiday celebrated in the *sukkah,* a latticed booth decorated with foliage, fruits and vegetables, traditionally erected outside the home and/or the synagogue. Friends and family gather in and around it to sing, play, pray and converse, and of course to feast.

The meals have a harvest theme: the bounty, color and taste of fresh produce.

Sukkos Dinner

Cantaloupe with lime wedges
Celery stuffed with egg and onion

Cold beet borscht

Turkey, with anna's stuffing
Mashed sweet potatoes in orange cups
Green peas

Spinach salad

Easy strudel
Fresh fruit bowl
Mixed nuts

Tea and sodas

Chanukah (Usually November or December). The Festival of Lights coincides with Christmas with decorations of the *Menorah,* or eight-branched candlestick and the Chanukah bush.

This is an historical holiday encompassing the story of a miracle, way back to l65 B.C. The King of Syria decreed that the Jews give up Judaism and adopt the ancient Greek religion. A rebellion followed. The five Maccabee brothers led the Jews to victory in the first war for religious freedom in history. When the Perpetual Light of the great temple was to be relighted, there was only enough oil for one day and runners were dispatched on the eight-day journey for more. Miraculously, the flame lived for eight days. Thus, the eight-day Festival of Lights was proclaimed.

It's a time for gift-giving and game-playing. Eat and be merry is the spirit of Chanukah, with no special regulations about food, but potato lotkes are a tradition because they are fried in oil.

Chanukah Dinner

Eggplant salad (caviar for peasants)

Mushroom barley soup

Shashlik david
Potato lotkes
Carrot tsimmis (without dumplings)

Banana nut cake with whipped cream
Pineapple slices

Hot apple and cranberry punch with cinnamon sticks and cardamom buds

Russian Tea Time

Russians drink tea differently from the tea-drinking British, who take it ink black with cream or lemon and sugar. But Russians make an event of it, too. We serve weak-to-medium strength, traditionally in a glass. To be very elegant and also to keep the fingers from being burned, there are silver or other metal containers for the glasses, often with filigreed patterns. I use crocheted coasters.

There is substantial food, and lemon wedges and jams for the tea, also apples are sliced right into it and eaten after dunking.

The part I couldn't manage was drinking it boiling hot through a sugar cube held between the teeth. I don't know how my mother and her friends did it without their tongues falling off.

Choose among these noshes or devise your own.

Egg and onion salad
Caviar for peasants
Cold rice pudding with whipped cream
Blini with hard boiled eggs and herring

Date nut bread, sliced thin, toasted and spread with cream cheese and jelly

Fruits and nuts

A Little Bite

I'm only going to tell you what my mother served to drop-in guests, which was quite frequent, for example, once a day at least.

But in those days, a circle of friends was more like family. They didn't stand on ceremony like we do today.

That custom nearly drove me crazy, but remember, she was spontaneous and I am a schedule person. However, I've loosened up in my later years and find it nice to have something in the fridge or freezer or on my shelf to offer someone on the spur of the moment.

Matzo Fingers

Stuffed baked Matzo Balls,
 hot or cold

Kasha varnishkes

Blintzes

Assorted savory breads,
 jams, jellies

Sour Cream and Minced Vegetables

Marble nut coffee cake

Raisin bread

Stewed prunes

Cold marinated salmon

Gefilte fish

Pickled fish

Light Dinners

1

Fish in vegetable sauce

Sliced cucumbers in
 Sour cream

Raisin cake
Sliced oranges

2

Meat and potato pie

Sliced tomatoes and cold
 broccoli salad

Cherry cake

3

Split pea soup, with
 slices of carrot

Cheese blintzes with
 applesauce

Date-Nut Cake

#4

Chicken Shticklach,
 with green vegetables

Beet Mandarin salad, with
 French mayonnaise

Poppy seed squares

5

Cherry soup

Shashlik

Poppy seed noodles

Jewel cookies

6

Tongue, crazy recipe

Steamed rice

Tomato and zucchini salad

Fruit compote

Breakfasts and Brunches

1

Pineapple juice
Fried matzo
Sliced tomatoes
Toasted bagels

Breakfast # 2

Fresh orange juice
Zucchini lotkes
Pickled fish
Wheat plus bread

3

Apple juice
Fried salami and eggs
Pickled vegetables
Marble nut coffee cake

4

Grapefruit juice
Scrambled eggs with lox
Beet and cucumber salad
Baked apple

5

Orange Izzy drink
Bagels, lox and cream cheese
Oatmeal nut pudding
Strawberries and cream

6

Baked half grapefruit
Breaded smelts
Poached eggs
Stewed figs

Light Lunches

1

Noodles and meat sauce
Lettuce and bell pepper salad
Toasted date-nut bread

2

Lima tomato casserole
Corned beef slices
Sliced papaya

3

Chicken pie
Lettuce wedge salad
Sponge cupcakes

4

Cold borscht and hot potatoes
Fish lotkes
Banana bread and lemon sherbet

5

Tuna salad on lettuce with
   pineapple slices,
   strawberries and
   cucumbers
Jewel cookies

6

Frankfurters and beans
   Sauerkraut
Beefsteak tomato salad
Peach pie

Information

Cooking Methods

Bread Crumbs: These are a snap to make with a processor—toast or let dry hard first. Or you can place in a bag and roll to make crumbs with a rolling pin. You can do the same for corn flake crumbs or graham cracker crumbs if you can't find these ready-made.

Carrots, to Shred: Use the largest size on your grater with holes about 1/4 inch. The smaller holes are for grating.

Chicken Fat, to Render: Cut off as much fat and skin as possible, cutting in small pieces. To about 1 cup of goop add 1/2 onion, 1/4 teaspoon salt and a pinch of pepper. Cover with water and simmer slowly until water is almost gone. This will take at least 1 hour, maybe even several. When the water has almost cooked away, watch carefully, stirring, until the pieces are crisp and brown all through and the water gone. The fat will crackle and pop and spit. A non-stick pan is best for this job, as the saucepan gets very messy. Cool and strain. Keep fat in a glass jar. Keep cracklings (*gribben*) separate.

To Cream: To mix until light and fluffy, usually refers to butter or shortening with sugar. The fat should be left out to soften, but if you forgot to take it out of the refrigerator, a good trick is to cut it into small pieces and work with your hands. The warmth of your hand will soften the mixture in no time and then you can use a spoon to finish mixing.

To Dredge: To coat lightly, usually refers to flour. This can be done by putting the meat or chicken pieces or whatever in a bag with a little flour and shaking it.

Eggs, to Hard Boil: Prick with a needle on the wide end so the egg won't leak out while boiling. Cover with cold water and simmer about 20 minutes. To peel, hold under cold running water while still hot. Then press the egg hard against the side of the sink and roll it around until the egg is cracked all over. The peel will come off easily. If you let the egg cool before you peel it, it will be a mess getting it off later.

Fat: If you need to measure butter or other solid shortening, pack it into the measuring cup, then hold the cup under hot water tap—so the water doesn't touch the fat—a few seconds. Plunge a knife into the center and twist and it will come out in one piece.

To Grate: Onions, potatoes and other vegetables can be grated with a hand grater on one of the small holes, depending on the texture desired, but of course, a food processor can do the job in seconds.

To Grind: To reduce food to very small particles by using a hand chopper or grinder, or best of all a processor.

Liquid, to Reduce: Boil on a high flame, uncovered, until desired amount is reached.

To Marinate: To cover with an indicated sauce called a marinade, for several hours or even days, according to the recipe.

Matzo Meal and Matzo Cake Meal: These come salted or unsalted, so you may want to adjust the salt in a recipe. If you can't find matzo cake meal, you can pulverize matzo meal in a processor. If worse comes to worst and you need some for certain Passover recipes, a mortar and pestle will work for small amounts at a time.

To Mince: To chop very finely.

Measurements: Although I made jokes about getting exact measurements from my mother's recipes in the introduction to this book, the truth is that they can't always be *exact*. Sizes will vary, temperatures will depend on differences in ovens, even the altitude at which you live will sometimes make a difference, especially in baking. So the best thing to do is to taste and adjust as you go along, and make your own changes right in the book.

Recipes, to Reduce or Increase: Many of the recipes in this book are designed to serve six people of average appetite. They are easily divided in half for three or in thirds for two people or doubled for twelve. But for more people, the flavorings, temperature and time may have to be adjusted.

To Roast: To cook with dry heat, usually in an oven.

To Simmer: When cooking food in a liquid, use a lower temperature than boiling point, or when little bubbles are formed and move gently.

Tomatoes, to Peel: Place in boiling water for about 10 seconds. Remove and immediately hold under cold running water for another 10 seconds. Remove core and peel. Skin will come off easily. Repeat if necessary.

Hints

Baked Goods: To test for doneness, insert cake tester or small sharp knife into the thickest part. If it comes out non-sticky, it's done. Another test for a cake is to press gently and if it springs back or has shrunk from the sides of the pan, it's done. For baked goods that have to rise, always preheat the oven and no peeking until it has baked for at least 3/4 of its baking time or it will fall.

Broth: When you don't have fresh broth, there are many kinds of bouillon cubes or powdered varieties available. Some, though, are heavy on the salt, so experiment. They usually take 1 or 2 table-spoons to a cup of water, depending on the strength you want.

Butter: If you need a little butter and it's in the freezer, scrape off sections with a vegetable peeler.

Cakes, Problems:
Too heavy: Mixed too much; too much fat or liquid, not enough sugar or leavening, inaccurate temperature.
Not risen high enough: Not enough leavening, inaccurate temperature.
Cake falls: Too much sugar, fat, leavening or liquid; not enough flour; not baked long enough; oven too cool; being jarred, e.g., stomping around the kitchen or bumping into oven; opening oven door too soon.
Tough crust: Too much flour; not enough sugar or fat; baked too long; oven too hot.
Top too cracked or rounded too high: Too much flour; not enough liquid; overmixed; oven too hot. An exception is that some loaf cakes should be a little cracked on top when done, for example, fruit cakes like banana-nut or date-nut cake.

Coffee Makers, to Clean: Using equal amounts of vinegar and water, let it go through one cycle. Repeat with plain water (distilled if possible). Rinse well before using.

Eggs, Sizes: My mother always used extra-large eggs but today's sizes may differ a little depending on where you buy them. The ones I used from a supermarket, subject to government grading systems, yielded 6 tablespoons per egg, right after being beaten. Eggs labeled large yielded 4.

Equipment: New kinds of equipment keep appearing all the time, especially the non-stick varieties. Some cooks have found that though they are convenient and less trouble to clean, they can affect the baking time. So you will have to watch carefully as you bake, experiment and adjust the recipes.

Fruit Stains: As soon as possible, hold the stained part tightly over a bowl and pour boiling water on it from a height of 18 to 24 inches. Sounds weird but really works.

Jars, to Open: Bang on its head, tap sharply around sides, turning, and/or hold under hot water.

Onions: To keep you eyes from tearing, peel under water. It's the volatile oil that makes trouble.

Oven Temperature: The safest way to regulate temperature is to test your oven with an oven thermometer. Electric ovens usually take a 25-degree reduction. Check this out carefully as most recipes refer to gas ovens. *Baking* success depends largely on precise temperature and timing. If your oven bakes unevenly, it requires professional adjustment.

Pies, General Method: If using a baked shell, use bottom shelf to bake so the undercrust will get done. General temperature is 450° for the first 10 to 15 minutes, then 350° for the final 35 to 45 minutes—but this can vary. Check toward the end and if it looks as if it's browning too fast, cover with a piece of aluminum foil. Fruit pies should have the fruit cooked well and crust not too brown. A glass pan takes a shorter time. Different types such as custard pies take a shorter time.

Pies, Problems:
   Crust too dark: Temperature too high.
   Crust doughy or too light, or filling underdone: Temperature too low or not baked long enough.

Pots and Utensils, Burned: Add 1 teaspoon baking soda to each quart of water and boil 20 minutes. Clean with scouring powder and abrasive pad. Repeat if necessary.

Sinks: To clean stains, use scouring powder that contains bleach. If stain persists, soak paper towels in bleach and lay on bad spots for 1 to 30 minutes.

Spices, Herbs and Other Flavorings: A little makes a big difference, so go easy, start with a small amount and add very gradually, tasting as you go.

Weights, Measures and Substitutions

3 teaspoons = 1 tablespoon
4 tablespoons = 1/4 cup
1 cup = 8 ounces
2 cups = 1 pint
2 pints = 1 quart
1/3 cup = 16 teaspoons

1 ounce = 2 tablespoons
16 ounces = 1 pound
8 ounces = 1 cup

METRIC CONVERSION: the following chart has the simplified, rounded out measurements generally used for recipes:

Volume

1/8 teaspoon	=	o.5 mL
1/4 teaspoon	=	1 mL
1/2 teaspoon	=	2 mL
1 teaspoon	=	5 mL
1 1/2 teaspoons	=	7 mL
3 teaspoons (1 tablespoon)	=	15 mL
1 1/2 tablespoons	=	20 mL
2 tablespoons	=	25–30 mL
3 tablespoons	=	45–50 mL
4 tablespoons	=	50 mL

1/4 cup	=	50 mL
1/3 cup	=	75 mL
1/2 cup	=	125 mL
3/4 cup	=	175 mL
1 cup	=	250 mL
3 cups	=	750 mL
4 cups	=	1 L

Weight

1 oz	=	30 g
4 oz	=	125 g
8 oz	=	250 g
12 oz	=	375 g
16 oz	=	500 g
2 to 2.2 pounds	=	1 kg

Baking pans—to substitute sizes

2 9-inch round pans	= 3 8-inch round pans
2 9-inch round pans	= 1 9-by-12-inch oblong pan
1 9-inch square pan	= 1 10-inch tube pan
2 9-inch loaf pans	= 1 10-inch sponge cake pan

Foods (amounts approximate)

Apples:	1 medium	= 1 cup, peeled and sliced
	1 pound	= 3 cups, diced
Bananas:	1 medium	= about 1/3 cup, mashed
Berries:	1 pint	= 2 cups
Bread:	1 slice	= about 3/4 cup soft pieces or 1/4 cup dry crumbs
Butter:	1 stick	= 1/2 cup or 1/4 pound
Carrots:	1 large	= about 1 cup grated
	10 medium	= 1 pound
Cherries:	1 pound	= 3 cups stemmed or 2 1/2 cups pitted
Chocolate:	1 ounce or 1 square	= 2 tablespoons cocoa plus 1 tablespoon butter or other fat
Corn flakes:	3 cups	= 1 cup, crushed
Cornstarch:	1 tablespoon	= 2 tablespoons flour (for thickening)
Cranberries:	1 pound	= 4 cups
Cream:	1 cup whipping cream	= 2 cups, whipped
Dates:	1 pound	= 2 1/2 cups pitted or 3 cups chopped
Flour:	1 pound	= 4 cups sifted
	1 cup cake flour	= 1 cup all-purpose minus 2 tablespoons
Garlic:	1 medium clove	= 1/8 teaspoon powdered or dry minced

Herbs:	1/3 to 1/2 teaspoon dried	= 1 tablespoon fresh
Lemons:	1 medium	= 2 to 3 tablespoons juice and 2 teaspoons grated rind
Nuts:	1 pound	= 1 1/4 to 2 cups, shelled
Onions:	1 medium	= 1/2 cup, chopped
Oranges:	1 medium	= 1/3 to 1/2 cup juice and 2 to 3 tablespoons grated rind
Parsley:	1 sprig, chopped	= 1/4 teaspoon dry
Peas:	1 pound	= 1 cup shelled
Potatoes:	1 medium	= 2/3 cup cubed or 1/2 cup mashed
Raisins:	1 pound	= 3 cups
Sugar:	1 pound	= 2 cups
Tomatoes:	1 medium	= 1/2 cup cooked
	1 pound	= 4 medium or 2 1/2 cups cooked

Emergency and Stock Items

In the Freezer

Freeze foods such as meat loaf or casseroles, ready to cook—or half-cooked in their own pans lined in wax paper or foil. When frozen, remove, wrap in more foil, label and return to freezer. When ready to cook, remove wrapping by immersing for a few seconds under warm tap water, then place in original container and bake or cook.

All items mentioned below freeze well. Sliced bread and cookies will thaw in 10 to 15 minutes.

Breads
Chopped raw onions
Minced fresh parsley
Grated citrus peel
Frankfurters
Salami slices
Blintzes, made small

Cookies
Pies, frozen in slices
Soups, frozen in frying pans—
   cook in same pans
Small matzo balls
Fish cakes, uncooked
Individual cheese cakes

In the Pantry

Cans or Jars:
  Herring
  Caviar
  Olives
  Pickled beets
  Pea soup
  Stewed tomatoes

Cherries
Apples, peaches
Gefilte fish
Tuna
Pineapple, crushed, sliced
Mushrooms

Dry Stock:

Matzo
Matzo meal
Matzo cake meal
Potato starch
Oatmeal, rolled and steel-cut

Barley
Noodles
Kasha
Corn flakes
Rice

Index